MINE EYES HAVE SEEN THE GLORY

Hamlin Alexander Coe

MINE EYES HAVE SEEN THE GLORY

Combat Diaries of Union Sergeant Hamlin Alexander Coe

Edited and with an Introduction by David Coe

Rutherford • Madison • Teaneck
Fairleigh Dickinson University Press
London: Associated University Presses

© 1975 by Associated University Presses, Inc.

Associated University Presses, Inc.
Cranbury, New Jersey 08512

Associated University Presses
108 New Bond Street
London W1Y OQX, England

Library of Congress Cataloging in Publication Data

Coe, Hamlin Alexander, 1840-1899.
　　Mine eyes have seen the glory.
　　　1. United States—History—Civil War, 1861-1865—Personal
narratives. 2. Coe, Hamlin Alexander, 1840-1899. 3. Michigan
Infantry. 19th Regt., 1862-1865. 4. United States—History
—Civil War, 1861-1865—Regimental histories—Michigan
Infantry—19th. I. Coe, David, ed. II. Title
E601.C67　　　　973.7'81 [B]　　　　74-5896
ISBN 0-8386-1492-2

PRINTED IN THE UNITED STATES OF AMERICA

Contents

Editor's Introduction

His name was Hamlin Alexander Coe. He gave his occupation as "wagon maker" when he joined the 19th Michigan Volunteer Infantry in August of 1862.

It was at the peak of the Union's effort to raise nearly a million men for the invasion and, finally, the defeat of the Confederacy. Every post office, city hall, and general store was flooded with posters and handout literature of patriotic content; town squares and city hall steps echoed to the blare of brass bands; and the lonely President still personally directed the major military strategy of the Civil War's opening phases—a burden he was later to turn over to General Grant, with great relief.

"Ham" Coe read the posters and listened to the brass bands and enlisted for three years.

He was sent immediately to the regiment's training camp at Dowagiac, Michigan. He was made a Corporal within the week and spent a brief five weeks at the camp, drawing equipment and clothing, "training", and sweltering in the August heat.

Ham Coe was barely 22 years old when he enlisted,

but, during the next three years of the toughest kind of infantry combat duty, he kept a daily diary that most vividly portrays the scenes—yes, and the sounds, tastes, and smells, too—of those cruel years. The diaries form the most compelling personal account of that, or any other war I have ever read.

The diaries lay, as such things will, in a trunk belonging to my father until his own death in 1966. It contained memorabilia of my father's life. Scrap books, hundreds of old, faded photographs, the family Bible —all the usual kept records of a lifetime.

Ham Coe was my grandfather, but I knew little of him, since he died in 1899, some 23 years before my birth.

It was nearly five years before I read the diaries in their entirety. Turning the musty pages of half a dozen pocket-size notebooks and unrolling the fragile and yellowed paper of the thirty-foot-long scroll was an experience I shall not soon forget.

Unlike autobiographies, or narrative accounts written long after the events, and colored by time, a daily diary portrays as accurately as it is possible what it was *really* like to be a Sergeant of Infantry in those tragic years when brother killed brother, and the United States of America very nearly failed to survive.

Ham Coe died in Stuttgart, Arkansas, in 1899, at the age of 58, his health eroded by the war years.

When he enlisted, Ham had an "understanding" with a small and pretty brown-eyed girl of 17 named Frances Ann Lacy. He refers to her as "F" in the diaries, and they kept up a constant correspondence all through the war. They were married less than a year after Ham came home—almost to the day that Confederate General Kirby-Smith surrendered his ragged army to the Union in Mississippi in May of 1865, finally ending the war.

Their marriage gave them three children. My grand-mother, Frances Ann, survived until 1917—18 years after Ham's death.

Ham must have hoped that his efforts to keep the diaries through every kind of adversity during the war years would have some value for posterity. He wrote in the last paragraph of his diaries:

> *Whoever should read my diaries for the years '62, '63, '64, and '65 will not criticize them, I hope, for they have invariably been written in a great hurry and often at great disadvantages, and, though brief and unmeaning to some who may read them, they contain a correct statement of my observations and actions while a soldier in the U.S. Army. . . . My wish is now gratified—that I could fight the battles of my country and return to my home to write the closing remarks of my soldier diary.*

MINE EYES HAVE
SEEN THE GLORY

The world will little note nor long remember what we say here, but it can never forget what they did here.

—ABRAHAM LINCOLN

GETTYSBURG: NOVEMBER 18, 1863

THE DIARIES

1862

Dowagiac, Michigan, September 14

Today I commence a diary of things and scenes as they transpire and meet my view while I am soldiering. I send this to you for your kind care and perusal, hoping at some future time to place the notes and items that I may make in my Journal. There is a portion of the time, I am sorry to say, that I cannot account for. It is the time that passed while in camp Rendezvous at Dowagiac. However, the 19th Regiment (of which I am a member) left the above named place armed and equipped for Dixie at 6:30 o'clock. We arrived at Niles just at dark. Here, for the first time, I ate supper from my haversack. Soon afterward I fell into a profound slumber from which I did not awake until within fifty miles of Indianapolis, Indiana. The land for the fifty miles was a level, clay soil. It looks like a pretty hard site to make a livelihood, but it seems there is a great deal of the land cultivated, and it is being cultivated quite rapidly.

EDITOR'S NOTE: *Ham Coe enlisted August 6 of the same*

year, at the age of 22. His training, obviously, was brief. He gave his occupation as "wagon maker."

Indianapolis, September 15

We arrived at this place at 9 o'clock this morning. Before we reached the depot we passed camps of regiment after regiment. Shouts of joy went up as we passed. Next came a long train of batteries, principally Parrot guns. I should judge there were two hundred of them. During the stay here there was a fine orchard directly opposite the train. The boys stole apples, pears, and peaches. After waiting until 10:30 o'clock, the regiment started for Cincinnati. We arrived at Lawrenceburg just at dark. The first part of the road was like that I have just passed over, a heavy clay soil, and under about the same state of cultivation. On nearing the latter place, though, the surface became very hilly. In fact, I thought it almost mountainous. From the time we struck the hilly country, we traveled one of the crookedest railroads at the greatest speed I ever saw or knew. After leaving Lawrenceburg a short distance, we crossed the Miami river, and then it was not long before the Ohio river hove in view.

The next moment, we were rolling along its Northern bank at a rate of about forty miles per hour. Darkness now began to gather around us, and I am unable to make any more observations while on the train. The distance to Cincinnati being but twenty miles, we will be but a few moments in reaching our destination.

Before reaching the Queen City, we passed two encampments of Home Guards. They greeted us with many a hurrah as we passed. Arriving at the depot in

Cincinnati at 7:30 o'clock, we alighted from the train and formed in two ranks preparatory to marching through the crowded streets for two miles. It was one continuous hurrah and waving of handkerchiefs, the whole distance to Fifth Ward Market. There were but few who were not wet with sweat. Here we found supper awaiting us.

We were hungry, and I tell you the cold meat, light bread and coffee relished well. As we passed out of the market house, the regiment was honored with the Chief Salute of Flags. We then marched a few rods to fifth ward Garden House for sleeping quarters, chose the softest white oak planks we could find for a bed, and we slept fine.

Cincinnati, September 16

I awoke bright and early, washed, and then began to look about me. To describe this building would be almost impossible, so I will mention only some of it's principle features.

It is composed of wood, but partially covered, is large and spacious, thickly set with evergreens and flowers which make it a great place of resort.

The regiment was again formed and we marched to fifth ward for breakfast. We had about the same this morning for breakfast as we had last night. I returned to quarters and wrote to "F", then went out upon the streets to see what sights I could see in the Queen City. There were too many things to note in this small book, so I shall have to retain them in my mind the best I can. At 3:30 o'clock we had marching orders. At 4:30 o'clock we were again rolling over the same road we traveled

The wagon maker became a soldier.

yesterday. All were wondering what we could be going back for, but it was not long before the boys knew their destination. The train stopped at Gravel Pit, and we camped upon the bank of the Ohio to guard Harrison's Landing or ford. We stacked arms and laid down upon Mother Earth for repose with nothing over us but our blankets.

EDITOR'S NOTE: *The beginning of the civil war found the North nearly as unprepared as the South. Fully 85% of the 200 Regular Army companies were guarding post on the Western frontier. At that time, three million square miles of territory were guarded by less than 13,000 men!*

The Union Armies, during the entire four years of the war relied, primarily, on volunteers, although some conscription was tried with little success. The Confederates, on the other hand, began conscription early.

In all, over 2,500,000 men served in the Union forces during the war. Many, however, enlisted for terms of only three to nine months. The number of men in the Union forces, therefore, probably never exceeded 1,560,000 at any given time. In contrast, the number of men who served the Confederacy is estimated at 700,000, and the largest number of men serving at any one time at 472,000.*

September 18

At two o'clock this morning the long roll was beat, and everything was in confusion. In less than fifteen minutes we were off at the double quick to the river bank where they had already commenced forming in line of battle, expecting every moment that the rebels would ford the river and attack us. But it proved to be a great scare, and I presume the enemy was not nearer than fifty miles from us. However, it is to be remembered that the Rebels are threatening Cincinnati at this time. The excitement finally subsided, and we laid down upon our arms the remainder of the night. Soon after we had laid down, it commenced raining and rained very hard. I hope now that we shall have some cooler weather, for it has been uncomfortably warm thus far. I arose early and went through with the routine of camp life. During leisure hours I washed and dried my clothes.

September 23

It was very warm again today, so much so that the boys suffered with the heat while on drill. The company

*Livermore, *Numbers and Losses in the Civil War* (Boston, 1901).

agreed to mess, each tent to do it's own cooking. I hope we shall fare better. Lieutenant Clark and I took a stroll this morning in search of butter. After going about two miles we about-faced and returned to camp without succeeding. He promises me I shall go again tomorrow.

September 24

There was a fine rain last night, and it was very cool and pleasant this morning. I had a splendid day for my rambles. After a good breakfast, (the first in mess, and by far the best meal I have had since we camped here) H.H. Pullman and I set out in search of eatables.

We directed our steps westward along the railroad until we met the pickets, when we turned our course northward over the hills. We first passed through the Hon. Scott Harrison's yard. (He is the son of old General Harrison). He came to the front door and talked with us and gave us a glass of cider, then bidding him good morning, we went on our way.

We immediately commenced climbing the bluffs, perfectly ignorant of where we were going. In fact, we cared by little. At last we reached the top of the hill. Being somewhat tired climbing the rugged cliff, we seated ourselves upon a log to rest. As we looked back, the scenery was splendid. First, was the railroad winding it's way along the foot of the bluff, seemingly just at our feet, although it was half a mile to the floor of the succession of hills.

Second, was the river, which was alive with little stern wheel steamers (the river is very low and will not admit of large steamers running up and down the river) transporting troops down the river to Louisville, Kentucky.

The old Harrison house.

Lastly, we could see several miles upon the Kentucky shore the hills and green fields of Dixie. Then, coming to an about-face and looking North, we could view parts of Ohio and Indiana. At the foot of the bluff (and the descent northward was very rapid) lay the Miami River with it's muddy waters passing swiftly by. Then, across the river lay the Miami flats, (of which I have so often read) covered with a wilderness of corn.

Upon the opposite side of the flats could be seen stately dwellings and fine farms, also the town of Lawrenceburg, Elizabethtown, and Mortonville. The scenery was too inviting to tarry long where we were, and in a few moments we had descended to the banks of the Miami. Finding a canoe moored to the shore, we jumped into it and soon found ourselves upon the opposite shore. We then started for the far side of the flats, distant two miles, and all the way it was one constant cornfield.

About halfway across we came to an orchard of good fruit. Of course, we ate heartily of the fruit, besides filling a basket. We arrived at the opposite side at noon and, for the first time since I left Dowagiac, I sat down to a table of good victuals. After dinner, the good lady gave us some butter and chickens and filled our canteen with milk. We got back to camp at four o'clock, tired enough, but a good night's sleep will make us all right again.

September 25

This morning I feel somewhat lame. I went on duty and before night, I felt necessity of rest. I retired feeling pretty ill, but hope to be better tomorrow.

September 26

I slept but little last night. I was no better than I was last night, but before evening the medicine I took had taken effect and I felt quite well. After dinner I wrote to "F".

EDITOR'S NOTE: *Frances Ann Lacy, the girl Ham married after the war, was just 17 when the diaries began. Ham was 22.*

September 29

This morning old Ham was himself again! About nine o'clock I started, in company with Charlie Stowe, to

Ham's beloved "F" of the diaries–Frances Ann Lacy in 1886

get some eatables for the Captain and Lieutenants. From camp we went due North over the hills to the Miami river. We found the people generally clever and liberal.

We called at a large brick house and told them we would like some dinner. There were two young ladies about the house that went about getting the meal. We had a tip top dinner. We stayed and talked with them some time. Then, buying a quantity of butter, chickens, etc., we started on our return. We reached camp after roll call, but we were out for the Captain and thus we got out of a scrape. After a little rest we got supper. Ham, potatoes, pickles, stewed peaches, bread and butter, and apple pie!

October 1

Today I feel somewhat better. Our company was on picket duty last night. I, being unwell, was left as guard of the Captain's tent. At ten o'clock we were ordered to strike tents and move across the railroad and camp on the heights, which was a sensible idea, for we can have some breeze there. Also, we shall have some shade to lie in when not on duty. After pitching tents, I strayed off over the hills till I came to a schoolhouse, the first I have seen in these parts. It is a poor excuse, being built of logs and surrounded by woods. After reconnoitering the premises and taking a little rest, I returned to camp.

October 6

All drilling is suspended today on account of the burial of one of our comrades. I have listened to the first sermon today that I have heard in camp. What time I have had has been spent with the sick, and I have ascertained some facts as to the attention the sick are having and have resolved that tomorrow I will exert my influence in their behalf.

October 7

Another one of our number has gone to his long home. After breakfast, I put on a haversack and started in pursuit of eatables. I returned at an early hour with chickens, dried fruit, butter and green peaches. Upon cooking them and taking them to the hospital, I was thanked from all sides, which paid me tenfold for my labor. Before night several of our company followed my example.

Evening: Our company was ordered on picket. I rolled my blankets and great coat and went with the company. After stationing the pickets, Lieutenant Easton and I went out upon a prospecting tour. First, we visited the tomb of General Harrison. It is situated upon a hill upon his old farm, and is built of limestone and cement.

The yard is decorated with all sorts of shrubbery, and, as the moon shone clear and bright, it presented a beautiful appearance.

Next, we visited his old log cabin, fast decaying. Next, we went into his old orchard, getting all the apples and peaches we could eat. Then, spying a hand cider mill, we made some cider and drank our fill. The next sight was the tunnel of White Water Canal. It is blasted through solid rock nearly one mile through the bluffs to the banks of the Miami. It was quite a curiosity, being the first thing of the kind I had ever seen.

Thus passed the night until three o'clock, when we lay down upon a large, flat stone to sleep. At early dawn, we returned to camp.

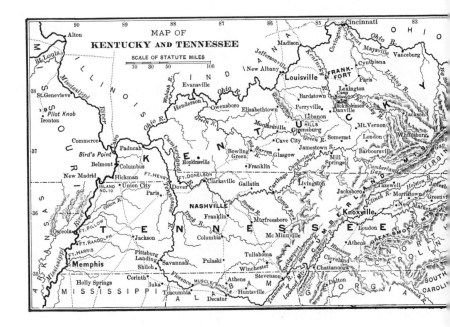

EDITOR'S NOTE: *Confederate Generals Bragg and Kirby-Smith invaded Kentucky at about the time of Ham's enlistment. They were defeated at Perrysville on October 8 and withdrew into Tennessee. It was to meet this ambitious Confederate threat that Ham's regiment was moving South from Cincinnati into central Kentucky.*

After the opening battles of the war in 1861, the Union's Western armies, of which Ham's regiment became a part, entered a period of buildup while the Eastern armies of both sides engaged in more active campaigns.

General Lee planned to invade Maryland, but was repelled

and withdrew into Virginia. Ham's regiment was moving,
along with hundreds of thousands of troops from their native
states, to swell the Western Armies.

October 13

This forenoon I did police work in camp. This afternoon, I passed the time in writing to Maria and Minnie.
Toward night it was rumored that we were to march the
next day. It was amusing to see the enthusiasm of the
boys and, when the order was read upon dress parade
that we were to leave the next morning, cheer upon
cheer was given which echoed and reechoed until the
sound finally died away among the hills on either side of
us.

Before sleeping, I wrote a few lines to "F".

October 14

At early dawn we struck tents, marched to the depot
and took seats in the car for Cincinnati. We arrived
there about twelve o'clock. The vineyards along the
Ohio shore were beautiful indeed, as the vines were
laden with fruit.

In short, it is a continual garden for a distance of
fourteen miles, and as we passed along we could see the
men, women, and children upon the side hill picking
grapes and gathering "garden sauce".

From the appearance of the fine, stately dwellings
along the route, one would naturally conclude that it
was a free state and the product of free labor.

Now, let's go back to the old camp and follow the
Kentucky shore to Covington. Like the Ohio shore, it is

hilly and broken and as yet is in a state of nature with now and then a cabin and truck patch to mar the scenery. It is a fact that there are very few frame or brick houses along the Kentucky shore from Camp Hooker to Covington.

Alighting from the train, we marched through the city for an hour or more. We crossed a pontoon bridge into Convington, Kentucky. After stopping at headquarters a few moments, *forward march* rolled along the line. Again, you could hear our low and heavy tread along the macadamized road. We marched directly in the rear of the town and camped in a beautiful grove of beech trees. We lay down upon the ground for sleep tonight. I tell you I slept soundly upon beech roots.

October 15

I awoke this morning about two o'clock after a sound and sweet sleep. I am pretty lame from yesterday's march, but as we are to stay here a few days, I shall be all right. At early dawn, we pitched tents, and it seemed like home to get our things in place and have the boys sit around and tell about the sore spots the march made.

After dinner I began to look around me to see what observations I could make. The first thing that met my view was the tented field laying between me and the town of Covington. There are thousands of soldiers here from all parts of the West. In short, the whole division is here waiting for marching orders.

Most of them, like ourselves, are new recruits, while a few are old regiments. On going among the latter, I found them ragged, greasy, and worn out with fatigue, though they were full of glee and merriment. My observations were next directed to the town of Covington.

It is rudely and irregularly built. Although there are some good buildings, they (like Cincinnati) are blackened and dirty from the smoke of coal that is used for fuel instead of wood. Still farther North, across the river looms up the Queen City. A dense mass of black smoke is all I can see.

Then, looking to the West, I can see but the high and irregular hills dotted with tents, swarming with soldiers. I am told that numerous batteries are planted upon those heights.

Now, seating myself upon the roots of a beech tree, I direct my eyes to the East. Oh! What a sight! About eighty rods in front of me runs the Licking River. Upon the opposite shore the bluffs rise almost perpendicularly to the height of 100 to 150 feet. They are perfectly barren.

Upon these heights are planted heavy siege guns. This forms the East and West defense of Cincinnati. There is a drill call, so I must go. . . .

After drilling a short time, we received permission from the Captain to let us go to the front and see the form of defense there. They looked like the rest upon the hills. Heavy cannon were mounted ready to pour destruction upon the enemy should they approach. Besides, there were three rows of rifle pitts, which swarmed with soldiers.

While on dress parade tonight, a courier came and brought the Colonel marching orders. When they were read, three rousing cheers were given by the boys on the Nineteenth. The boys are running to and fro through the camp, wild with excitement. They think little of the toils and fatigues, or the long march that awaits them.

October 17

I have been upon battalion drill this forenoon. I have passed the afternoon in Covington, and went to the Tavern and had a warm meal. After returning, I mailed a letter to "F".

October 18

We arose early, packed knapsacks, and prepared for a march. We waited anxiously until one o'clock, when the Colonel ordered the tents struck, and we were soon on the move. We have made ten miles this afternoon, passing through a broken and uneven country, but very wealthy.

October 19

We camped last night in an amphitheater. We arose at seven o'clock. We have marched seventeen miles today to the town of Crittenden. I have thought that I have been tired, but never so tired as I am tonight. The boys confiscated some hogs, sheep and chickens, and since eating a good supper I feel better.

My observations through the day were many and varied. I have time to note only those of the most important. The country, like that of yesterday, is uneven, owned by *Capitalists* and well cultivated. So far, the Union sentiment has been very faint indeed. I don't believe there are twenty-five Union men in the whole distance we have traveled.

From what I could learn of the inhabitants, almost

every door was thrown open to Morgan and crew, when
he passed this way about three weeks ago. One thing I
noticed was that the ladies were the first to greet us, or
wave the handkerchief. This is the same place that Morgan camped while threatening Cincinnati.

Confederate General John H. Morgan

EDITOR'S NOTE: *Morgan's Raiders, led by Confederate General John Hunt Morgan, were a mounted cavalry force of
2,500 men. His men plundered, stole horses and destroyed
bridges. His most famous escapade occurred nearly nine months*

after Sergeant "Ham" Coe's first mention of his band of raiders.

Authorized by the Confederate Command only to lead a raid into Kentucky, he crossed the Ohio river on July 8th, 1863 into Indiana. Panic seized Indiana and Ohio. The militia was called out and Union cavalry started in hot pursuit. Attempting to get back across the river to the Confederacy, General Morgan was forced into battle and lost 800 of his men. His force fled up the river, but surrendered on July 26, 1863. Morgan was taken to the state penitentiary in Columbus. On November 26th of the same year, he escaped to the Confederacy.*

October 20

This morning the Brigade was ordered to Falmouth, and our course has been due East over one of the roughest roads I ever traveled. The country is very hilly and uneven, but little cultivated. The people are of a poorer class and more loyal by half. The most of them belong to the Home Guards.

Today we have traveled but fifteen miles. Coming to a little muddy creek, we halted for the night. We possesed some honey, sheep and chickens. Ahem! Southern honey and soft bread aren't such a bad dish for a soldier after all. Tonight I shall rest my weary limbs upon a bed of cornstalks.

October 21

At early dawn we resumed our march over the hills and along the beds of creeks to Falmouth. We reached

---

*Collier's Encyclopedia, volume 14 (New York, 1960), pp. 152-53.

this place tired and footsore about three o'clock. The Licking River at this place is so low that we crossed it without even wetting the soles of our boots.

Falmouth will compare very well with Adamsville by leaving out the grist mill and saw mill. It is important only as a strategic point for the defense of the Kentucky Central railroad, by which provisions and stores are conveyed to the advance or front. I am told we are to stay here a few days. For my part, a little rest will be acceptable.

October 22

This forenoon I washed my clothes and had a general cleaning up. I tell you we were a dirty set after marching in a perfect cloud of dust for four days. The remainder of the day I have been writing. We received mail tonight for the first time since leaving Covington.

October 25

The assembly call was blown very early this morning, and the low heavy tread of infantry with music playing told us but too well that the right of the Brigade was under way. In a few moments *Forward March* rolled along our line, and we were again in motion going directly West.

At an early hour it commenced raining. I find my large rubber blanket quite a protector from the storm. About ten o'clock we emerged from the hills and woodland upon a macadamized road. The remainder of the day we passed through as fine a country as I ever saw.

We arrived at Cynthiana quite late and camped a little

North of town. The place doesn't amount to much, and if I may be allowed to judge, is a *Secesh Hole*. I was upon rear guard today and camp guard tonight. What a night! It snowed and blew all night. In the morning the snow had fallen to a depth of nine inches. The inhabitants tell me that the like has not been known for years. While I was mounting guard, marching orders were issued, and in twenty minutes tents were struck and the line formed, ready and eager to go and thus sooner reach the heart of Dixie. Poor fellows, they little think of the long road that is ahead of them.

October 27

We started at an early hour this morning for our destination (Lexington, Kentucky) but after going through the beautiful town of Paris, the Brigade was ordered to halt and wait further orders.

Paris is a pretty and well-built place. It is built mostly of brick. As the Brigade passed through we were welcomed from every side. Flags and handkerchiefs were waved, and there was a constant cheer from our boys. After pitching tents, I passed time lying upon my blanket.

October 28

This morning we were again ordered forward, and today we have passed through the most beautiful parts of the country I ever saw. Stately mansions—they look more like ancient palaces than anything I can compare them to—large and beautifully decorated yards, etc. Also, large fields of grain met our view upon either side and as far as the eye could reach.

On nearing Lexington, I noticed several fields of hemp, the first I ever saw growing. We passed through but a small portion of the city upon our way to camp, which was nearly three miles West of the city. As soon as we had stacked arms and unslung knapsacks, Oliver and I started for the nearest house to get something to eat. We found people quite wealthy.

After eating a good supper, we returned to camp. The boys had pitched the tents and we have comfortable quarters for the night.

October 29

We are camped in a walnut grove close to water. Upon the whole I am quite pleased. There are countless numbers of troops encamped about us from all parts of the West, and they are still coming. The beautiful country still extends as far as the eye can reach. There is a grist mill close by and the boys proposed to get some meal and have some mush. I tell you, it tasted good!

November 10

I have been very busy and withal a little negligent the past ten days, so that I have not kept up with my notes as I should have done. However, I think there is no harm done, for there has nothing of importance transpired, but the routine of camp life. My leisure time has been spent as usual in reading and writing.

I am Corporal of the Guard today at Division Headquarters. On going to camp for dinner, I found Oliver overhauling a box of provisions he had just received from—I don't know whom. The piece he gave me tasted good, however. I wish the somebody a long life of happy days for the piece I ate. I have returned to headquarters and to duty. Toward morning, Jim Hoffstatter and B. Harris milked two stray cows that were close by, while I pulled an armful of chickens, and we are now waiting for the relief guard.

November 12

The day is a very pleasant one. I have passed the time very lazily until near noon, when it was rumored that we were to forward march again tomorrow. After dinner, I passed the guard and directed my steps toward the cemetery. The first thing that attracted my attention was the Henry Clay monument. It is a round column of marble, ninety feet in height, and based upon a structure of limestone and cement. At its top is his profile carved in marble and lifelike both in size and looks. There are other monuments here, but none so large as Clay's. There are some beautiful ones, however, and they look to me as though they might have cost quite a sum of money.

Another thing I noticed is that the ground is laid out in circles of from 15 to 30 feet in diameter, and the bodies are buried with feet towards the center circle, so that tombstones are all in a circle upon the outside. The grounds are covered with flowers, etc. Upon returning to camp, I found Charlie quite ill. I have worked diligently for three hours to get him into a sweat but have not succeeded. I am afraid he is going to be sick. Orders were read upon dress parade to prepare for a forward march tomorrow.

EDITOR'S NOTE: *By far the largest number of deaths on both sides during the Civil War were caused by illness of one kind or another–chief among them were typhoid fever and pnuemonia. Of the total of 560,000 deaths on both sides during the four years of war 185,000 men were killed or died of wounds, while 375,000 died of illness of "other causes."**

November 13

At early dawn we were upon the march. We have traveled eighteen miles over a good road and through a splendid country, halting at Nicholasville, Kentucky. This place is a sort of one-horse town. It might have been called a city in Wildcat times. The buildings are old and dilapidated. The inhabitants seem to have so little enterprise about them. We are now in the very heart of Kentucky, and I wish I could always live in as pretty a country as this. If there were free labor here and free institutions of learning, the state could not be excelled. But here they pay from $20 to $30 per quarter for schooling, and hire negro labor for $50 to $100 per year; and the inhabitants tell me their labor is dear at that, for they have to stand over the eternal nigger with a club to make him do anything. I have stood the march today better than any day since we started. We have pitched tents and carried straw about two hundred rods for our beds. I shall sleep well tonight.

November 14

I passed the day in camp. Michigan money is good

*Livermore, *Numbers and Losses in the Civil War* (Boston, 1901).

here today, and we are having lots of good things to eat. Charlie had to go to the hospital today.

Union Hospital in a barn

December 5

Early upon the morning of November 15, I was taken with a severe chill. A high fever followed, and from that time to the present date I have been perfectly insane. Upon inquiring into my case, I find I have been having the pnuemonia and typhoid fever. I have had the best of care (for a Hospital) by both surgeons and nurses. I find I am very weak and emaciated, but if I am careful it will be all right with me in a few days. The surgeon says he is going to send me to camp tonight. Upon coming to my reason, I found Charlie in the same room with me, but he has not been so sick as I have. Still, he is very sick. His disease is more of a lingering nature, but good care, I think, will bring him out of it, for he has a good appetite and good countenance.

December 8

Wid came last night to care for Charlie. You may bet we made the old tent ring with joy. I hope that Charlie will improve somewhat faster. I have taken a room with Wid and Charlie at a private house (Mr. Bronaugh's) and I hope that I too shall improve in health somewhat faster.

December 10

Charlie was no better this morning. If anything, he was worse. I have walked to camp and back again today. It is almost too far for me to walk, but I must see the boys.

December 11

Being weak, I feel somewhat tired, as I have waited upon Charlie for the last twelve hours; but a little rest is all that I require. Charlie is, in my opinion, decidedly worse. I was in camp today, and the boys told me that they had marching orders for tomorrow.

December 12

I was at camp early this morning to see the boys start. They had already struck tents and were anxiously awaiting the orders to move. They started before it was fairly light. I wish I were able to go, too. Charlie is worse this morning. There is no dodging it now.

December 13

Poor Charlie expired this morning at seven o'clock. His sufferings and trials as a soldier are ended. He has gone, I hope, to a better world, where wars and rumors of wars are not heard. As for myself, I am tired and almost worn out, but rest is all that I require. The pleasant weather still continues. It seems more like spring than winter.

December 17

As I get my regular sleep now, I am recovering more rapidly, but not so fast as I would like to. There has been another sick soldier brought here today from the 85th Indiana by his father (Mr. Geiger), but he is a convalescent, he will need but little care.

December 19

A clearer and prettier day never dawned. The sun shines as clear and as bright as summer, birds are singing, and it seems like spring. The old gentleman (Mr. Geiger) is taken sick this morning with the erysipelas. After waiting upon the sick, I went down town and loitered about until dinner. Upon returning to Mrs. B.'s, I found Mr. Geiger worse. I apprehend he is going to

have a pretty hard time of it. I have been writing all afternoon. My eyes pain me pretty badly. Otherwise I am
doing well.

December 21

I have been waiting upon Mr. Geiger all day again
today, and tonight I am almost tired out. He is so heavy
and perfectly helpless that it makes it worse for me than
it would be otherwise. It is hurting me, but I cannot see
him lie there and suffer and so far from his friends, too.
I have but little hope of him.

December 24

I am lame and tired, but Mrs. Bronaugh has procured
the services of a darky for the sick ones, so I shall be
relieved of my labors; but the old man is bound I shall
stay with him and see that all goes well and give him his
medicine.

December 25

Christmas today and oh, how gloomy and lonely, far
from home and friends, among entire strangers, and in
charge of two sick ones. The kind lady got a splendid
dinner and has tried to make the day as merry as possible for me.

Mr. Geiger is surely failing. He cannot last much
longer. I have spent part of my time on the streets to
take some observations. I noticed it is a great day for

the niggers—the town is full of them, some tight, some singing, others dancing. I could only now and then see a white man and he is a soldier. The more I see them, the more I pity the cause of freedom that is about to be proclaimed. We do not want them among us at the North, and certainly such an ignorant and brutal set as I have seen today cannot take care of themselves. I shall patiently await the future to see how the matter will be managed. The only peculiarity I notice in custom here is, when persons meet, the password is *Christmas Present*, instead of *Merry Christmas*.

December 26

Mr. Geiger died this morning. He suffered everything last night. I was up with him most of the night. I have passed the day in resting and writing.

December 27

I have passed the day in various ways about the house—in reading and mending my clothes, and tonight in writing. I am mending, but slowly, very slowly. My eyes are very weak yet. I hardly know what to do for them.

EDITOR'S NOTE: *On the morning of December 31, 1862, 180 miles to the south of Ham's convalescence in Nicholasville, Union General Rosecrans engaged General Bragg in a fierce battle at Murfreesboro–some 25 miles south of Nashville–which was, for all practical purposes, a draw.*

There were terrible losses, however, for both sides. Both the Confederate and Union armies each lost over 9,000 men killed or wounded. The Confederates, in addition, captured about 3,700 Union prisoners.

*After Murfreesboro, both armies went into Winter quarters.**

December 31

It is anything but pleasant this morning. The wind and snow are blowing, and it is quite winterlike. I have passed my time in reading the daily news and writing. There is stirring news among the troops today, and I apprehend we shall have some fighting to do soon. Thus ends my career for the year of 1862.

*Geer, *Campaigns of the Civil War* (New York, 1926), p. 205.

1863

January 1

Upon the new year, it is said, "Turn over a new leaf." I have thought of it several times through the day, but I cannot find my book. It has been a long and lonesome day. I have been wandering about all day, and more than once my mind has wandered homeward, and I have been reminded of the pleasures and pastimes of one year ago. How I wish I could enjoy this bright moonlight night as I did then. In its stead, I am in the town of Nicholasville, Kentucky, among entire strangers. All day I have been wandering about with folded hands as if in search of some unknown object, but I have been awake to the transactions of the day. I will relate them briefly. Early this morning the streets were thronged with vehicles of every kind and a great many on horseback. About ten o'clock the public sale of horses commenced, lasting until noon. After dinner commenced the hiring out of negroes. They are hired for from $50 to $125 per year and are to be clothed and given medical attendance in the bargain. I noticed some that I thought were tough bargains. There were some private sales of negroes, but nothing that attracted attention in that line.* I have had a good dinner at Mr. Bronaugh's and helped the steward draw rations for the hospital. Since supper I have been writing home and reading the news of the day. Thus ends the New Year. As a holiday it is but little thought of by Kentuckians.

January 7

This morning I had a chance to go to Regiment. It was a good long road to travel. At ten o'clock, the ambulance was ready, and I took leave of the hospital. About five miles out we came to a vineyard. We came to a halt and had a draught of wine. Then on we went again for seven or eight miles at mule speed over a good road and through a beautiful country until nearing the Kentucky River, when the surface became uneven and hilly. Upon nearing the river, it became almost mountainous. The bluffs rising almost abruptly to the height of one hundred to two hundred feet. The road wound around the hills, and at times it was blasted for a half mile upon the side hill, thus making a road upon and in the solid rock. After crossing the river, the same scenes occured. Then came the tableland. This is splendid, too, but of no great extent, for we soon came to Dix River, which like the Kentucky River (only not so large) has bluffs of lime rock for banks. After emerging from the hills of the river, we soon came to Camp Dick Robinson, of which we have read so much. All there is to mark the

*Attractive Negro women or especially intelligent Negro men were sometimes offered at private sales.

spot are some half torn down barracks, old wagons and cannon; but on we went thru as pretty a part of the land as before to Danville, Kentucky. I reached General Beard's Headquarters at sundown pretty tired, but we had a good supper, and I am going to have a good place to sleep, so tomorrow I shall be all right.

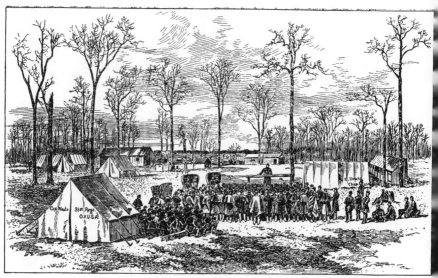

Camp Dick Robinson, Kentucky. Sunday Preaching

January 8

I arose early this morning, and after breakfast I set out to observe what I might in the city. I found it a beautiful place of about 5,000 inhabitants and well built brick. I noticed, too, there of several institutions of learning. The Male Guard would not let me go in and see the several principals, so I made my way to the Provost Marshal's office where I found William Huff. We had a good time, of course. After dinner, I strapped my knapsack on my back and started for camp. I found the boys all right, and we had a joyful time. Thus passed the day.

January 14

As I awoke this morning I found that water was dripping in great drops upon my bed. The storm has continued all day without cessation. The old tent leaks badly. It is a poor place for me, but I shall have to stand it. I passed the day in the usual way, reading and writing. Take it altogether, it has been a lonely day.

January 16

It is anything but pleasant today. I have kept indoors pretty closely, and we had a great time trading and trafficking among ourselves. I bought a revolver of Eph.

January 17

Today it is more pleasant and I have been to town and had a good dinner and all the Porter I could drink. On account of the storm, the mail has been delayed and we have nothing to read, so I have passed the leisure time playing checkers.

January 24

Saturday has come again and with it a rumor that we are to march to Louisville. I have passed the day cleaning my gun and writing.

January 26

At eight o'clock this morning we started upon the contemplated march. We have passed over a rich country but rather uneven. We have marched about fifteen miles. I am pretty tired. The road has been muddy, and about three o'clock it commenced raining and we have had a lovely time pitching tents. I saw one natural curiosity today—that was Cave Spring. It was upon the north side of the hill and in under a projecting rock, which perfectly protects it. The water was splendid. We passed through the town of Harrodsburg, which is quite a place. We are now encamped four miles from Harrodsburg.

January 28

Early this morning we were on the move. The country is like that of yesterday and day before yesterday. About noon we passed another spring. It issued from the rocks upon the north side of the hill, and I think it was the best water I have tasted since I left Michigan. In fact, it was a complete fountain. We marched about the same distance that we did yesterday. I am not so tired today. I got in with one of the Post Teamsters and rode all I wanted to. But tomorrow the First Brigade goes ahead, and we will have to do some tall marching.

January 29

We arose early, and at sunrise we were on the move. Our course has been northwest. The country is a little more uneven, but still it is rich and well cultivated. We have marched twenty-three miles and are now camped fifteen miles from Louisville. I have ridden most of the day, so I feel first rate. We passed through several little towns today, but they don't amount to much. In fact, I saw nothing worthy of note.

Union troops on the march

January 30

At daylight this morning we were under motion. As we had to go but fifteen miles to Louisville, it was soon traveled. At twelve o'clock we were encamped in full view of the city. The country that we passed over today has been almost a dead level, the soil very rich and extensively cultivated. Upon nearing the town, it was a complete garden spot for three miles. The whole distance from Danville to this place (eighty-five miles) has been made in four and a half day. I feel pretty sore and lame, and there is not much prospect of time to rest, because we are to go down the river soon. The remainder of the day I shall pass writing.

January 31

I had thought we would stay here a few days to rest, but before the sun had arisen in the clear eastern horizon, we were ordered to strike the tents and prepare for a march. We have marched the distance of five miles to the landing and are now embarking upon the "Ohio No. 3". At twelve o'clock Company E is nicely quartered in the cabin and now expect every hour to go down the river. So far as the City of Louisville is concerned, it is scattered over a great deal of ground, but outside of the heart of the city it doesn't amount to much. The business part of town is nicely built upon a single street, extending along the river probably four miles. It is protected by rifle pits and embrasures, but I did not have time to examine them throughly. From what I saw of them, however, I should judge they were not as formidable as those of Covington and Cincinnati. The whole division is now embarking. We are having some fun, as well as confiscating some good eatables.

February 1

We have lain at the wharf all day. We have had a big

time through the day running around the town of Portland. The boys pulled pies, cakes, bread, etc. It has taken longer to load than I expected, and we have not left the wharf yet but probably will in the morning.

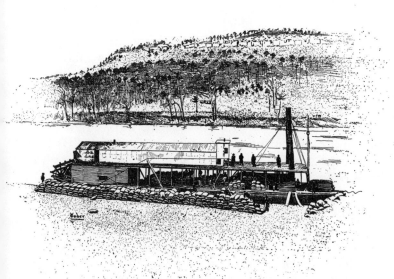

"We lay at the wharf all day."

February 2

We lay at the wharf all day awaiting orders. About three o'clock the expected message came, and we were soon steaming down the Ohio. It being very cold, I could not be out on deck to make any observations, so I returned to the cabin, concluding that the comforts of a good fire were preferable to the cold wind upon the hurricane deck. The forenoon I passed as I did yesterday.

February 4

I did not sleep much last night, the old boat trembled and squeaked so. About two o'clock we came to the mouth of the Cumberland River. The boat hauled up to the landing for coal. I went down and helped them load. At this place the Colonel received a dispatch stating that they were fighting at Fort Donaldson and urging this regiment forward with all haste; but nine gunboats and fourteen transports have gone up the river already. I think the contest will be decided before we can reach the Fort.

At four o'clock in the morning we were again under-way and plowing the waters of the Cumberland. It is still cold, and there are some indications of a storm, but I have been out enough to ascertain that this part of Kentucky and Tennessee is generally level along the river, and but little cultivated. The only thing that marred the thickly but poorly timbered shore was occasionally a log cabin and adjoining truck patch, and they were generally negro huts.

About sundown we hove in sight of Fort Donaldson. All we could see of it in passing by were the earthworks and trenches. As we passed by it was ascertained that the fight had ceased and that it was a complete victory for our side. The forces engaged were about six hundred on our side and about six thousand of the enemy.

About a mile above the Fort we came upon the fleet, and ran to shore. The boys all started for the battlefield, but I feel too poorly to run around tonight. There are all sorts of rumors afloat concerning the fight, but I cannot credit all. I hear everyone is frantic with joy over the victory.

The Cumberland River from Fort Donaldson

EDITOR'S NOTE: *A year previously, the Union Armies under General Ulysses S. Grant's first real command, at the age of*

39, attacked Fort Henry and Fort Donaldson with 17,000 troops.

It was one of the Union's first ineffectual blows at the Confederacy. When President Lincoln's call for more men came in April of 1861, Grant was earning a poor living in the leather trade at Galena, Illinois. He was a graduate of West Point, but by 1861, Grant was a "broken, dissipated man for whom no one would have dreamed of predicting a brilliant future."*

February 5

As the day closed with a snowstorm yesterday, the marks of the battle ground are not as plain as I wish they were. Enough can be seen, however, to satisfy me. The dead horses marked the plain distinctly. The ball holes in the houses, too, plainly showed the desperation with which both parties fought.

One hundred and fifty dead of the rebels have already been buried, including two Colonels and one Quartermaster. Our losses were thirteen killed. There were a good many wounded upon both sides, but I did not go to see them. I saw some of the prisoners. It will suffice to say that they were poorly clad, dirty, and overbearing in conversation.

EDITOR'S NOTE: *Exactly a month later, "Ham" Coe became a Confederate prisoner himself!*

February 7

This morning the sun broke forth over the lofty

*Geer, *Campaigns of the Civil War* (New York, 1926), pp. 51-53.

heights clear and bright. As the fleet was under motion all night, the morning found us quite a way from our starting point, and there were quite extensive marks of civilization this morning. Although the river banks at times rise almost abruptly to the heigth of one hundred fifty to two hundred feet, the land is inhabited and cultivated heavily.

Towards night the city of Nashville hove in view, but the banks were so high and so thickly built with storehouses that I could see but little of the city. Passing up above the bridges (the railroad bridge is in ruins) the boat moved to the landing where we shall stay the night.

February 9

This morning we slung knapsacks and marched through a small portion of the town (by the way, it is nothing but a mud hole) to camp. After going about three miles, we halted upon a beautiful little lawn as I have ever seen close to a pretty little spring and a brook. There are a great many troops here, but they are going daily to the assistance of General Rosecranz. It seems like home to get into the tent again.

February 15

I have felt rather poorly the past few days and have neglected almost everything, but nothing of interest has transpired until today. We have received new guns. They are the Enfield rifles of English manufacture. They are light and neat.

February 21

Early this morning we struck tents. Taking the macadamized road to the South, we traveled about nine miles and camped at a little place called Brentwood. It is simply a way station upon the railroad. The face of the country is level and extensively cultivated.

February 22

Company E is upon picket duty today. It is cold and windy, so much so that when sitting around the fire we could freeze upon one side and roast on the other; but we went to work and built a hovel (such as we used to build for the sheep at home) which was quite comfortable. We had little to eat, but plenty of good water to drink, which distilled through the rocks.

February 23

Before coming off picket this morning, Jim, Delos, and I went in advance of the post to get some straw to take to camp. While there, an old darky came along with some dried peaches, and we made him shell out. He was rather reluctant about it. About ten o'clock we were relieved and went to camp and have spent the remainder of the day in rest and hunting gray-backs,* but as before, I have found none.

This afternoon there was a brigade celebration in honor of Washington. We were addressed by the Colonel of the several regiments. There was music by the

"Gray-backs" were lice—the "cooties" of the Civil War.

brass band of the 22nd Indiana. We also passed several resolutions and had a good time. Thus passed the anniversary of Washington.

March 2

A prettier morning never dawned than this. I passed the forenoon washing my clothes and playing ball. At an early hour this afternoon, we were called upon battalion drill, but just as we got into the field, we received marching orders. We returned to camp, struck tents, and were upon the way.

About nine o'clock we came to a halt and camped. It being a dusky moonlight, I could not see much as we passed along the road. The country was very hilly but well improved. The distance traveled has been nine or ten miles.

March 3

Upon waking this morning, I could see the town of Franklin a little way to the front. About ten o'clock Companies E and C were ordered out upon a foraging expedition. Procuring some hay and corn, we returned to camp. I saw nothing of note upon this trip but uneven ground and stone.

EDITOR'S NOTE: *At the time of Ham's capture, General Grant with 75,000 men was preparing to attack Vicksburg. His forces were on a front some sixty miles long with the center at Holly Springs, Mississippi.*

In the spring of 1863, Ham's regiment was a part of the

forces traveling south by river boat to join General Rosecrans'
forces on Grant's left prior to the terrible Union defeat at Chick-
amauga. As it turned out, Grant's successful capture of
Vicksburg—together with the Union victory at Gettysburg—became
the turning point of the war.

Chickamauga, in the Indian tongue, means "Valley of
Death." More than 32,000 men were lost by both armies at
Chickamauga, by far the bloodiest battle of the war. Perhaps
Ham's capture before that battle, in which the remains of his
regiment fought, was providential for Ham.

March 5

We met the rebs again. The artillery duel commenced
at nine o'clock A.M. and by eleven o'clock the fight became general. We fought until three o'clock P.M. when
overpowered by numbers and completely surrounded by
three lines of battle, we were obliged to surrender. We
were then marched to Columbia under guard, a distance
of eighteen miles. Darned if I'm not tired, but I hope a
night's sleep will make me alright.

March 6

Last night we stayed in the courthouse. The floor was
covered with rubbish of various kinds, to say nothing of
the offal that was mixed with it. However, William,
Oliver, and I got close to a window, through which we
got the fresh air from without and managed to sleep
soundly, which relieved me greatly. At nine o'clock P.M.
we were marched one mile from town, halted and
searched for side arms and received scanty half rations
of bacon and cornbread. This done, we resumed our

Near scene of Ham's capture, Franklin, Tennessee

march, went but a few miles and camped for the night. It has rained almost continously today and bids fair to continue raining all night.

March 7

It rained all night again, and we got up this morning wet to the skin. At an early hour, we resumed our march. After a hard day's tramp over rocks, through mountain gorges and winding creeks waist deep and still rising by the constant rain, we arrived at the place (Louisburg) and are quartered in a school house for the night, which from outward appearances has been a very

fine institution, but is very much delapidated now. It is
built of brick, is three stores high, and has the appearance of having once been well furnished.

March 9

At ten o'clock we were again upon the march but did
not go a great ways. We are encamped in the woods. It
is raining very hard, and a dreary night awaits us with a
bed on mud and water.

March 10

We got up this morning soaking wet, and ere the day
had fairly dawned were ordered to fall in and resume
our march. We arrived at Talihoma just at night after a
hard day's tramp through rain and mud. We have
waded a dozen or more streams above waist deep, and
tonight are encamped in the open air without a stick of
wood to make a fire by, with which to dry our cold, wet
clothes. It is very cold. The boys that stand this are
really "Iron Sides". Great God! What suffering awaits us
next?

March 11

It rained all night, and we are wet and cold. A good
many of the boys are sick this morning, and no wonder
they are. We were marched to the Provost Marshall's office early this morning and stripped of our great coats,
blankets and canteens per order of General Bragg. We
were then put on board a hog and cattle train bound for
Chattanooga.

The car affords us little or no protection from the storm, but we shall avoid some hard marching. We are suffering very much from cold, exposure, and hunger. There is a general murmuring among the boys cursing the man that stole their clothing. I believe if there is such a place as hell, and if curses will send a man there, there is no reprieve for General Bragg.

However, we all hope to get out of Rebel hands before long and then—! Towards night I traded the old watch Father gave me to one of the cursed Butternuts for a blanket, and if they do not steal this from me I shall make myself quite comfortable the remainder of the journey. God knows, it will be hard enough at that.

March 12

We arrived at the place (Chattanooga) late at night and were quartered in a new building intended for a hospital (by the way, it is anything but a pleasant or cheerful place for a sick soldier). There is no one but a tired, weary, and emaciated prisoner of war that can enjoy the pleasures of such a hovel.

At four o'clock P.M., we were put on board the train again bound for Bristol. I have amused myself through the day by stealing pies, gingerbread, and peanuts from the peddlers that throng the place and have made it pay very well, too. I have a full haversack now to eat from.

March 13

We are running at mule speed over the rough, uneven tracks. We changed cars at Knoxville.

March 14

We arrived at Bristol at five o'clock P.M. About three o'clock P.M. we came to Holster River. The bridge had been burned but a short time before by the 2nd Michigan Cavalry. Where will this regiment be next? They either have a fight or a horse race every day! We have a good camp ground tonight, but it is raining very hard, and we shall pay another gloomy night without a fire or a bite of anything to eat.

March 15

We have remained here all day simply because the Colonel in charge of us is religious, and it is against his principles to transact business on the Sabbath; but he can get drunk and fight without smiting his conscience a bit.

I have amused myself as I did at Chattanooga but did not make it pay as well, for the pies I stole I could not eat, and I am hungry enough to eat almost anything, too, but I can't go a "mail clad" pie. It has commenced raining again tonight, but I have slipped the guard and got into a box car, where I will be secure from the storm one night more.

March 16

At three o'clock P.M. we were on board the train again bound for Lynchburg. Today, the same as other days just past, we are plodding our slow and weary way to Richmond.

March 17

We arrived at Lynchburg at twelve o'clock noon and were quartered in a church for a few hours. We were then removed to the fair grounds, where we had the horse and cattle shed for shelter.

This afternoon I stole some apples. By thunder, they tasted good. The boys are tired sick, and worn out, but I feel very well. I tell them I haven't time to be sick now.

March 19

We were again loaded on the cars bound for Richmond. It has rained all day and is getting colder fast.

March 20

Early last evening it commenced snowing, and about twelve o'clock midnight the engine gave out, and the train has been standing upon the track ever since. The snow is about eight inches deep.

We have nothing to eat, but the boys are bound to keep warm if they can find rails to burn. We have cut some boughs from the scrubby pine and cedar that grows along the rocky hillside for bed, and were it not for being so hungry I should be quite comfortable tonight.

March 21

At five o'clock P.M. we were relieved from our anxiety by another engine but this one could not start the train, so the boys got off the train and ran it by hand about eighty rods. We have had nothing to eat yet and a poor prospect of getting anything very soon, but with plenty of fence rails to burn we have managed to keep warm.

EDITOR'S NOTE: *The infamous Confederate Libby Prison, in Richmond, Virginia was an old tobacco warehouse hastily confiscated to house Union prisoners after the battle of Bull Run in 1861.*

Later, in Ham's time, the prison was used as a temporary depot for prisoners who were enroute to exchange points—an arrangement between the North and South which collapsed in the fall of 1863. Ham's luck still held ! During his confinement at Libby Prison, Ham made only a single entry, whether because his diary was confiscated, or because of his health we do not know. That single entry, however, tells vividly of the conditions the prisoners endured, as well as the rapidly degenerating state of the Confederacy.

March 22

Early this morning we arrived at Richmond and were marched to Libby prison where the boys, as well as myself, were glad to seek a resting place. Many of the boys sank down upon the floor (unable to support themselves longer) from exhaustion and hunger. As we passed up the stairs, they gave us some blankets. About every third man got one.

About ten o'clock A.M. and five o'clock P.M., we received about three ounces of bread and the same of stinking meat, which is all we have had to eat. Do they mean to starve us ? But I guess it is best for us to eat but little.

During this journey we have suffered greatly from incessant rain or snow, our clothes wet most of the time, and while upon the train outward bound from Lynchburg we were banked up in the snow and remained there forty-eight hours without anything to eat, but we had plenty of good dry rails to burn and thus kept warm. Our provisions upon the whole route have consisted of rotten and maggoty bacon and corn bread. The bread was made from meal that had not been sifted, mixed with water, a little grease from the stinking bacon and no salt and baked in an old iron bakette or upon a board in front of the fire. The Rebels claimed they were giving us half rations, but I have received at no time as much for three days as we did within our own lines for a single meal.

There was once we got plenty of US crackers—that was at Chattanooga. We got once or twice wheat bread made as the corn bread was.

There are none but the toughest of men that can keep alive with such usage; but the Guards (Mississippi) divided their rations with us. They appear to be gentlemen in every respect. Their officers too were gentlemen and courteous. They allow us a great many privileges we did not expect to receive at their hands.

The country we have passed through is anything but prosperous. Everything seems to be going to destruction; buildings and fences upon whole plantations burned and torn down. No crops growing, no stock to graze upon the now green and growing grass. The inhabitants tell me that they do not know where their next year's supply of meat and bread is coming from for their individual wants, to say nothing of supplying their army. They say they have no cattle, no hogs, no horses, and that they have been stripped of everything that would be of any use to their army. God knows they must have something to live upon in this rocky region. I have found several people in the South who will take U.S. greenbacks for their commodities before they will their own money.

Date Unknown

From March 22nd to March 31st, we were confined in Libby Prison, which is a large brick building. Our company was put upon the third floor with the 85th Indiana. It was a gloomy time. We were furnished rations twice per day. At each time we got about three ounces of musty wheat bread and about the same of rotten corned beef. About one half the time we got soup in place of beef, which was none the more palatable.

Upon the night of the 29th I was taken sick, but luckily for me it was not so bad but what I could navigate, and upon the morning of the 31st at two o'clock, we were called up to go within our own lines.

I picked myself up, though rather poorly, and Oliver helped me to the train. I really thanked God when we arrived at Richmond, but I thanked everybody when we arrived at City Point, within our lines, where I could receive proper medical treatment.

We arrived at City Point at noon and embarked upon the *State of Maine* for Annapolis, Maryland. At six o'clock on the 31st we hauled to at Ft. Monroe. It was too dark for me to see much of the fortress, but still light enough so that I could see some of the defensive works. I felt too weak to go ashore, and examine them and thus lost a grand sight. About twelve o'clock at night we shoved off, expecting soon to reach our destination.

"We arrived at City Point at noon."

During our stay at Ft. Monroe, we drew one load of bread, some boiled ham, and hot coffee. I never had anything taste so good as it did then. Some of the boys made themselves sick, too, by eating too much.

On the morning of April 1st, we arrived at Annapolis, and Jim and I started for the hospital. We found a good room, containing three beds that look neat and clean, where we shall stay until we feel better than we do now.

I had a good scrub and wash all over, put on some clean clothes that were free from vermin, and went to bed. I rested good, but Jim is pretty hard up. I hope a few days will suffice to make us both all right once more. "As long as there is life there is hope."

June 22

It has been some time since I have written the transcriptions of the day. There has been nothing but the monotony of hospital life to wile away the lonely hours during my stay here, so I will merely make a statement of scenes and incidents.

Up to the 19th of April I spent most of my time with Jim, at which time he died. Poor fellow, he departed this life without a struggle and, I hope, has gone to a better world.

Upon the evening of April 18, I was taken sick with typhoid fever, but luckily I succeeded in breaking up the attack, and so kept about the room. Simultaneously, I was attached with sore eyes, and that give me a tough one. I was confined to a dark room for some time, and at the present time I cannot see half as well as I used to. I have thus been deprived of my only source of enjoyment, reading.

This hospital is the Navy Yard buildings fitted out for the sick and wounded. It is built entirely of brick and will accommodate about four thousand patients. The yard is splendidly laid out and set with all sorts of flowers, evergreens, fruit and forest trees, and the institution as a hospital is carried on upon scientific principles and is really a home to the tired and weary soldier. I would to God that every soldier in the field could enjoy what I have here—quiet, plenty to eat and drink, and a good bed and room to occupy.

There are three monuments in the yard that were erected in memory of several seamen that nobly fought and bled for the birthright of our country. Among other curiosities that attract one's attention in passing through the Yard is the cable that the Rebels stretched across the

James River as a blockade. It is made of wrought iron two inches in diameter and double linked. To look at it, it seems as though it was heavy enough to break of it's own weight.

This Navy school was founded by James K. Polk in the year 1845. Connected with this hospital is the St. John's College hospital. That is controlled by the ladies principally, and is a splendid affair, if anything excelling the Navy yard hospital.

I have visited the capitol several times, but aside from the old state house there is scarcely a thing worth notice. It is true that there is a great deal of wealth in the place, but there is no enterprise or industry. In short, it is a place noted for wealth, and the principal citizens live here and do business at Baltimore.

The town is small, built principally of brick. The streets are very narrow and there is scarcely a shade tree to be seen. A more irregularly laid out place I never saw. The new state house is quite an imposing edifice. It is large, built of brick, and it's cupola or belfry is one hundred fifty feet high. The boys say they can see the Potomac river, distant forty miles, from it's top. I presume I could if my eyesight were good. There are several large churches too that are fine specimens of architecture, but the greatest curiosity of the place is the old state house where General Washington resigned his commission in the army and retired to private life. The rooms remain just as they were then, the same furniture and pictures, with the old library, etc. A man is kept there on purpose to conduct visitors through the building and see that nothing is meddled with.

In front of the building stands a tree that General Washington planted with his own hands, and it has grown to be six feet in diameter. I forget the name of the tree now, but the boys called it "The Tree of Liberty."

The next and last thing of any importance I will mention is a gun that was captured, but the English sank it in St. Mary's river and it was afterward taken out. It is some twelve feet long and twelve pound caliber. It is a mere popgun, compared with the cannon that are used in the present war.

June 23

I arose early and prepared to depart. At ten o'clock we took passage on the steamer *"Favorite"* for Baltimore and were obliged to wait patiently until three o'clock P.M. for the start. But after a pleasant ride we arrived at Baltimore at eight o'clock P.M. We went immediately to the Union League Relief station for supper, which consisted of light bread, ham, and coffee. We finally lay down upon the soft side of a brick pavement for repose. At two o'clock I got to sleep and slept soundly.

June 24

As it was quite dark when we entered the city, I could not prospect much, but early this morning we set out for the train that is to convey us northward. In so doing we passed about one and one half or two miles through the city, the streets of which are barricaded with stone and everything that could obstruct an invader's progress. Everything betokens the presence of the military, with the early prospect of an attack from the Rebels. At nine o'clock the train started, and we were rolling northward.

The first thing that attracted my attention was a living fountain. It's waters were forced to the height of twenty or thirty feet.

We arrived at Harrisburg at three o'clock P.M., stopping only long enough to change engines. The country was hilly and even mountainous the whole distance.

The citizens had turned out in mass to fortify every hilltop and soldiers were flocking to the standard from all directions, expecting every day to be attacked by Lee and his Rebel hordes. Baltimore was beyond my expectations as a town. It is a large place, built entirely of brick and very compact. Harrisburg fell short of my expectations. It is irregularly built and very much scattered.

June 25

As I awoke this morning I found we were rolling along at lightening speed toward Pittsburg, at which place we arrived at two o'clock P.M. The Union League here gave us another meal. It consisted of bread, butter, crackers, cheese, cookies, pickles and coffee. We then went on the train and are now on our way to Columbus, Ohio.

About forty miles from Pittsburg our train ran off the track, throwing the engine, tender, and two cars down a bank of twenty feet or more. There were two or three of the boys bruised some, but none seriously hurt. Today I have seen nothing but mountains, some of them so high I had to look twice to see the tops of them. They are covered with a thick short growth of all kinds of forest trees. At six o'clock P.M. we were again seated in the cars and were soon on our way.

June 26

This morning found us well on our way. About ten o'clock A.M. the passenger train just ahead of us ran off the track and made a general smashup, and our train was obliged to wait for repairs.

While we were thus waiting in suspense, I met an old farmer who invited me to go home with him for dinner. The invitation was too tempting to refuse.

Upon arriving at his place seven or eight girls met us. The old gentleman introduced me as a hungry soldier. The girls proceeded to get me some dinner, while I talked with the father and mother. The old folks stayed in the sitting room while I went to the dining room to dinner.

I had a splendid meal with the girls, and I noticed I took a long hour to eat; but the girls could out talk me, there were so many of them! They had three brothers in the army, and I had to tell them all about my captivity, etc. It was really like home.

At three o'clock P.M. the train was again on the track, and I bid my hosts goodbye. Soon we were again making 2.40 speed towards Columbus, where we arrived at seven o'clock P.M.

Passing through the city, we halted under a tree, spread out blankets, and took lodging for the night.

June 29

In Columbus, I went before the Board of Surgeons for an examination. They pronounced me unfit for duty and are going to send me to Detroit for further examination. I found Moses Tice at this post hospital, and had a good long talk. He is the same chick that he was when he waited upon me in Nicholasville, Kentucky.

July 1

I drew rations. While thus engaged, I came across William Stevens, and passed the time in conversations with him.

July 4

This morning I procured a pass and went to Columbus, thinking to find the "4th", but I was sadly disappointed, for I saw nothing but strange faces in the many streets that thronged with busy beings of both sexes and of all classes.

It seems so strange to get into a crowd of Union people once more. One would step up to me and ask me if I would not have something to drink; another would ask me to dine with him, and another to smoke a cigar.

The ladies, too, seemed to be courteous in the same patriotic cause, and I received numerous invitations from them to tea, and to finish up a lady asked me to go to a dancing party; but I declined the invitations from them and went to quarters.

I arrived at camp just as the boys had supper ready, but having eaten so many knicknacks, I could not eat.

The city of Columbus is rather a nice sight for an inland place. It is neatly built of both brick and frame dwellings. The streets are well shaded and watered. Nearly in the center of the town, is the state house, which is a large building of hewn stone with a large dome and lookout. The yard is large and well set with shade trees, but as yet they are quite small.

I have passed the day rather pleasantly for a soldier, but when I think of the happy hours I passed on the last 4th and the comparatively short distance that separated me from the dear ones that were the light and life of my enjoyments one year ago today, I can not but feel sad and lonesome. I can imagine that I see Cousin Phil fixing the wreath of roses for sister's head before she was to enter the ballroom, and how beautiful she was. I remember, too, how neat and tidy Francis appeared as she glided through the gay and mirthful circle of smiling faces. Little did we think it was the last hours we were to chase with flying feet for a time.

Then, Cousin Minnie and Phil seemed to enjoy the pastime and bid defiance to dull care and trouble. While these scenes of past pleasure have been flitting through my mind, I must confess I have been a little lonesome, but before another year passes by I hope to be with those associates and loved ones, again to enjoy the pleasures of real life.

In the evening the boys in camp sent up a few sky rockets and Roman candles. Thus ends the 4th of July.

July 22

For two days I have done nothing but make the best of life in my present situation. Reading has played out with me again, and if my eyes fail as fast as they have for a few days I cannot write. At four o'clock P.M. today we were called out to receive pay. I received $104.00. It is now sundown, and a more drunken set I never saw then Company K, 1st Paroll Forces. During the evening

I went to Franklin and bought a satchel, pocketbook and pocketknife.

July 23

This morning an old Dutchman came after me to go and build him a hayrack. I was glad of an opportunity to get away from the drunken crowd and have taken the job. I have worked all day and I never was so tired as I am tonight, but I have had plenty of good victuals and the ladies to talk with. I worked in the shade of the house, so I had a rare chance. I would work until I became weary and then go into the parlor and talk with the fair ones.

July 24

I have finished my job today and received $1.25 for my labor. I have had as good a time as I did yesterday, though I was too lame to move only when I was obliged to.

Towards night, an old lady came along and made me promise I would build her some gates. She said she had plenty to eat and did not care if I did not work more than half the time, but unless I feel better than I do now I shall stay in camp some time.

August 1

Up to this date nothing has transpired worth recording, simply the routine of camp life to wile away the long and lonely hours. Drunkenness, theft and profanity have been the ruling motives since payday. In their drunken rows, men are shot, stabbed or unmercifully bruised without cause or provocation. During the past week my eyes have grown worse quite fast. The doctor has burnt them with caustic and nitrate of silver until they are very dim. If I have to stay here much longer there will be no help for them.

This morning a company of us clubbed together, hired an omnibus, and concluded to have a pleasure ride and thus to pass some of the lonesome hours. We went in a southwest direction toward Dayton. Going about five miles, we came to a church where there was a funeral in session. We stopped and attended the funeral, and I think I never saw a more solemn occasion. There was hardly a dry eye in the congregation.

The corpse was a child of about two years, and I think I never saw anything more beautiful or innocent. Adjoining the church was a grove where there was a picnic in session. Our attention was drawn in that direction next.

It was nothing more nor less than a militia muster, though there were plenty of ladies upon the ground who set a bountiful table. We had a good dinner and a good time until one o'clock, when we ascertained that there was another picnic about four miles beyond, so we started for it. We found them enjoying themselves in pretty much the same way that they were at the first, but there was one thing that had a tendency to mar the pleasures of both parties. That was that the girls all seemed to be sad and lonely. They really seemed to seek solitude. They would get together and sing some national ballad and the next moment would be wandering off two by two and take seats in some carriage to pass the time alone.

On our return to camp we stopped at a tavern, where the boys drank beer, sang, talked and, in short, had a regular soldier's spree. I had a good excuse to get out of the drinking crowd. My plea was that it would hurt my eyes. The boys let me off without a murmur. I returned to camp at sundown, went to the boarding house, where I have hired board for a week, and ate supper. Thus ends the day, and I am tired enough, but I have had a good time for a soldier.

August 27

Since Father was here I have kept no diary, partly because I have been negligent, but more particularly because I gave Father my diary when he went away and consequently have had none until today and shall now endeavor to be more punctual in my duties.

I have passed the forenoon in Columbus. I sent for a book, *The History of the War for the Union*, and bought some paper and envelopes. I passed the afternoon in camp.

As to the time previous to the above writing, it has been very monotonous, nothing to do and nothing to pass the time only to listen to someone read the Daily and wander around to hear whatever I could. There appears to be considerable sport in camp, but of a discordant nature between Guards and Parolls.

August 28

Today I have been ordered to take command of Company K, 1st Paroll Forces and have entered upon my duties. Towards night I received Muster Rolls to fill out preparatory to pay. I am glad to have something to busy myself with, and if my eyes will do their duty until I can make out the payrolls, I shall have a good berth.

September 20

Again I am obliged to record my negligence in writing in my diary, but so monotonous are the transactions and scenes of this camp that it matters little. Nothing has marred the routine of our camp life since my last writing but the pay table, and that has only increased the vices and folly in camp. Occasionally I see a new shirt or, hat, that illy contrasts with the person who wears it, but as a general thing the soldier's money goes for poor whiskey or some frivilous thing that is gone in a few days. The greater part of the day I have spent in Columbus and have had quite an exciting time. Several times we met Butternuts and came almost to blows as often. About noon a fire broke out in a dwelling, which caused some excitement but did very little damage. The next attraction was the funeral of an officer.
Evening: Before I had rested from my visit to Columbus, a friend from the hospital came and urged me to go home with him, distant two miles. I finally consented to go.

Our course lay first toward the Sioto river to Camp Todd, where we distributed some medicine to the invalids (and a sorry lot they are); then our course ran Northward up the river. Passing about one mile of the beautiful valley of the Sioto, we came to a dam across the river. crossing upon it and ascending the opposite bank, we came suddenly upon his rude but pleasant home, where we met the smiling countenances of his father, brother and sister.

This visit was a treat to me, for of all the places I have been yet none have seemed so much like home. We talked long and fast until ten o'clock, when the pie, cake, peaches, etc. were passed around, and then started for camp, but not until they had wished us success with a solicitation to come again. We arrived at camp at twelve o'clock, tired enough.

EDITOR'S NOTE: *Ham refers in the next entry to the Union's disastrous defeat at Chickamauga which shook the people of the North almost to despair.*

At the time of the entry, the battle of Chattanooga resulting in one of the most strategic victories of the war for the North was still two months in the future.

September 26

Another week has glided away, which has been rife with rumors that we are to join our respective regiments for duty. The late battles of the Cumberland Army have aroused the people to the fact that reinforcements are needed, and everything is ordered to the field that can use a musket. For my part, I am willing and ready to go and do what little service I can. It will relieve me from the idle and monotonous scenes of camp life, and usher me into more exciting and beneficial duty to my country, and now I am impatiently counting the time until we shall take our leave from this place.

September 27

Another Sunday has passed, and I have occupied my

time more beneficially than is usual for me. Early in the
morning I did some Company writing, then, producing
a pass, in company with D. L. Higgins proceeded to Columbus for the purpose of going to church.

Out of curiosity we wended our way to the Catholic
church, but finding it very much crowded we concluded
to retrace our steps. When we passed the Baptist church
the goodly people were just congregating. We came to a
halt, right-faced and entered the house of God, where
we were greeted with "How do you do, Soldier" from
several ladies and grey-haired veterans.

The sexton escorted us to conspicuous seats where all
could view the soldiers. There was no representation of
the blue coats in the house save my friend of the 42nd
Illinois, and myself, consequently we had many a gaze or
rather a kindly look fixed upon us, as well as being
noticed several times by the minister in his discourse.

I had several speculations in my mind as to what their
thoughts be, for long ago I had thought that all mankind
looked upon every soldier the same—tempted upon all
sides, he was prone to wander from the paths of virtue
and morality and being absent from friends and social
circles would grasp the passing pleasure, whatever it
might be, to divert his thoughts and thus forget the
happy days that had passed and gone and with it forget
the teachings of fond parents.

Such were my thoughts, and really, I thought myself
among civilization (as I term it) once more. Oh! If I
could only see those with whom I am acquainted con-
gregated together as I have seen strangers today before
I go to the bloody strife of battle, I should be satisfied.

After retiring from the church, we proceeded to a
saloon, had a dish of oysters, then returned to camp
with the determination that, if I remain here until
another Sabbath, I shall go to church again.

I have forgotten to mention our stroll after church. At the junction of High and State streets we agreed to take a stroll to the eastward. Passing the state house and General Mason's headquarters, some half mile farther, we came to the lunatic asylum which is the largest I have ever seen of the kind and, I think, as pretty a yard. Upon the different streets we saw stately dwellings, beautiful yards, etc. I was forced to the conclusion that there is much more wealth in Columbus than I at first thought. Withal it is a rather pretty place.

October 9

We have turned over our muskets today, and all exchanged men are ordered to be furloughed for ten days, which caused a great excitement and stir in camp. Of all the manifestations I ever saw among soldiers either in camp or out, I never saw any like that which exists in camp at the present time. It is all hurry and going to and from headquarters, and more noise cannot be made by mortal man.

October 10

I received my furlough today, or, rather, bought it, and am homeward bound upon the next train!

October 22

During the last thirteen days I have not written in my diary, and I can only ask myself, who could spare the precious time with friends and home to note the transactions of the day. I do not wish to be understood that the events of the last thirteen days have entirely run away with my mind, but I have seen too many friends and have had too many good times to once think of writing. And now I think it almost impossible to enumerate all the pleasures and pastimes that have flitted by so swiftly, so I will only mention the route.

I went first from Columbus to Urbana, then from Urbana to Clyde, Ohio. The country and improvements upon this trip have been far superior to anything I have seen in my travels for the last year.

I found the folks at Clyde all well, and spent the time very pleasantly until Tuesday, when Maria and I started for Michigan, where we arrived Wednesday morning. I found the good people all well. It was go here and go there and plenty to eat and drink, and I think I enjoyed those hospitalities if ever a fellow did in this world, and, too, I think the soldier is the only person who can enjoy the pleasures of home and friends. Long will I remember the few days that have just passed and gone, so I will leave this page a blank and trust the scenes and incidents to my memory.

October 23

This forenoon I have washed and had a general cleaning up and have been ordered to the field. I am to start this afternoon. I am in a poor plight to go, but there is no reprieve, so I must pack my wet clothes and get ready for the start.

Three o'clock found me seated in the cars headed for Cincinnati, where we arrived at ten o'clock in the evening. After some looking and tramping, H.H.P. and I put up for the night at the Dennison House. It being dark the most of the way from Columbus, I could make few observations. But the Queen city, I find the same as one year ago, thronged with busy men and women engaged in the pursuits of life, liberty, and happiness.

October 24

The program of our journey has changed, and we are going to Louisville by railroad instead of by steamer as originally planned. I have run all around the city and have seen too many things to enumerate upon this page. One thing I must mention, however. I have ridden upon a street car today for the first time. In short, I have enjoyed myself first rate. I should like to be here on next Monday, as General Rosecrans is to be here, and the people are intending to give him a grand reception. I anticipate a long and lonesome ride tonight.

October 25

We arrived at Jeffersonville at twelve o'clock last night. The night was quite frosty. Being tired and weary upon our arrival at Jeffersonville, we sought the first shelter for sleep. A covered wagon chanced to be in our way and favored us with it's protection. There Sgt. Hills of the 51st Illinois, H.H. Pullman and I slept soundly and sweetly until late in the morning.

We then found our way to the City Hotel for breakfast. About eleven o'clock we crossed the Ohio River by ferry to Louisville, Kentucky. We are now quartered at the Soldier's Home (I style it hog pen) until further orders. This soldier's home is situated on Broadway between Eighth and Ninth streets. It is built in the form of barracks, in short is a regular hovel. Although I have traveled through this city before, I find it extends further and is more regularly laid out than I had any idea at first. It is closely and neatly built, but the streets are not improved as they are in the northern states. To be brief, we are getting into Rebeldom again in earnest. We are getting southern society at least, and how different are the habits and customs of the people. God only knows where I shall stay tonight, but methinks they will have a good time keeping me at this soldier's home. I prefer the shelter of some friendly tree to this place.

October 26

I did sleep in the barracks last night, but it was by the coaxing of the other boys.

The people of Louisville appear to have forgotten or rather revived from the desolations of war, and business seems to be going on with redoubled energy. In short, everything seems to be thriving.

I went to the post and drew a rubber blanket and canteen.

October 27

At seven o'clock this morning we were ordered out and took seats in the cars for Nashville. There were two train loads of troops, and we had all sorts of noises and sport.

Our course has been via Munnford, Bowling Green and Cave City. As a general thing the country has been rolling and fertile, though poorly cultivated. Though the fact that the country has been laid waste by the armies of Bragg and Buell fully accounts for the apparent sluggishness of the farmers. Scarcely a fence is to be seen, and many are the buildings that are deserted or destroyed all along the road from Louisville to Nashville.

We arrived at this place about eight o'clock P.M., went to a coffee house, bought a cup of coffee, some bread and butter, and ate our supper. Then we went to the barracks and bunked for the night. It is a tough place, but I guess we can stand it for a night or two.

October 28

Upon awaking this morning I find myself on the fourth story of a large brick building, feeling rather the worse for wear. The building we occupy as barracks has been confiscated, is new, not more than half completed, and contains about five hundred rooms and is filled from basement to garret with anxious, uneasy soldiers, waiting for transportation to their regiments.

Indeed, there is quite an army within these walls. There are at least four thousand souls cooped together. Some are singing, some dancing, some passing the time over a deck of cards while there is no small number engaged as I am writing the passing events and to their friends at home, and, too, there are countless numbers of the more reckless cursing the red tape of the officers for not sending them to their regiments, and I don't know as I can blame them.

Still, we are now nearly to the front where we must expect to obey all orders and be commanded by commissioned officers. In short, we are appreciating the realities of war once more.

October 29

We were awakened this morning by the guard and received the order to fall in with cheers, and again marched to the depot. Once there, we were placed upon the tops of freight cars to be sent farther toward the front. We arrived at Murfreesboro at nine o'clock A.M., and learned that our regiment had gone some forty miles farther to the front, but, as fortune or luck seems to favor me sometimes, it seems to now, for Company C is here with a train for provisions, and is going out tomorrow, but as the regiment is about forty miles from this place, we will be nearly two days getting there, and I dread the journey.

October 29

I have passed most of the day sitting or lying upon my knapsack for rest. I know I am missing a grand sight of the battle field of Stone River and the fortifications that surround Murfreesboro, but I am too tired to prospect. It is now nearly twenty days since I had a full night's sleep, and tomorrow I have a march of forty miles to reach the regiment, and from the way the boys tell it would not surprise me if we had a brush with the guerillas before we reach our destination, but I must sleep tonight and have taken quarters in a deserted house for that purpose.

October 30

By daylight we were on the way with a slow but sure

"We arrived at Murfreesboro at nine A.M."

progress through the valleys and over the hills, and it rained a constant storm.

At noon, the train stopped, and we confiscated a hog and had a dinner upon hard tack, fresh pork, and coffee. By this time we reached the mountains, and indeed the scene was quite natural. The hard day's travel over, we halted in an open field for the night. It has rained all day, and bids fair to rain all night, but I have got under a roof that will partly shelter me from the storm and that is all. My clothes are wet and 'tis cold, but here goes. I must turn in and make the best of it.

The Union Armies assembling for the attack on Lookout Mountain

EDITOR'S NOTE: *During this time General Grant's Union forces and Bragg's Confederate forces manuevered in preparation for what was to be the battle of Chattanooga.*

In the same period, over 4,000 rebels deserted to the Union side. Confederate Generals Bragg and Alexander both attributed the massive desertions to "The enemy marshalling his forces in plain view." Alexander remarked "The sight was a grand and impressive one, the like of which had never been seen before by anyone who witnessed it."*

Geer, in his Campaigns of the Civil War *says "This was the only battle of the Civil War in which the topographical con-*

*Geer, *Campaigns of the Civil War* (New York, 1926), p. 324.

ditions were such that the defenders were in a position. . .which could look down upon the hosts of the enemy (30,000 men) forming for the attack, and it was too much for the nerve of the Confederate soldiers, who were as brave as any on earth."

In addition to the deserters, 2,000 Confederate prisoners were taken.

November 2

I have reconnoitered the most of the day, and I find this place very beautiful and wealthy, withal it is picturesque and sublime. It would require the historian or artist to give the village a just description.

McMinnville is so romantic, but like a great many other towns of the south it has been demoralized and more or less destroyed, and, too, I heard and saw one thing that is entirely ahead of my time, or rather behind the age. It is this—the ladies (as they are styled) have a box of snuff and a little stick that they insert into the box and then chew it. It is a nice way of using tobacco that they have in this country. I find it a very common habit among the women of this country, and I have never been more surprised than when I learned the above to be a fact. It shows me very plainly the industry and especially the intelligence of the people. I shall conclude by calling them a regular set of fools.

November 3

I have been detailed today to write in the Provost Marshall's office and have entered upon my duty. As at Camp Chase, I am very busy, and it is very tiresome to sit all day at the desk, especially upon my eyes, but this is the only duty I can do, therefore, I am bound to do it.

November 7

This is another of those delightful days so common in this climate. We are high up in the mountains, and with the pure air and bright sunshine we really enjoy the day. Business was quite lively until twelve o'clock, when it was reported that the Rebs were upon us at least two or three hundred strong, and naught can be heard now but the marshalling to arms of the battalion, and all is excitement, not excitement either, but rather preparation for battle. Although I doubt their attacking us, they may give us a salute. God protect the right. I only wish I had a gun and accoutrements, so I could go into the scrape. It is all in the future yet, however, and it won't pay to worry until I hear some report of artillery or small arms, and then I can find something to do.

November 9

For the past two days I have been writing very busily. The Rebs concluded not to come close last Saturday, so we did not get a shot at them, and some of the boys were disappointed. Upon such occasions I find the old 19th awake and ready for a fight. At the sound of the bugle, every man was at his place, some of them with their coats off as though they were going to chop wood. The forage trains get bushwacked almost every time they go out. In fact we are surrounded by Rebs and Bushwackers, and between the two enemies we have some warm times.

November 16

I have had little time in which to write to friends or look about me, but the Captain was relieved from this office today, and I presume I shall be too, and I am glad of it, for it is a tiresome job. All that I dislike about it is having to leave good quarters.

I was surprised on first doing Provo duty to find that the chewing of snuff was a very common habit among the ladies of Tennessee. I would not believe it at first, but every day I see them parading the streets with their little sticks in their mouths. I will not speak disrespectfully of them, however, for who knows—but what I shall place my affections on one of these birds and become one among them, and, too, my feelings of hatred of them arise more from shame than hatred, so I will rather take a lesson from them. I notice, too, they have another very common habit that I thank God I have not yet formed, that is drinking strong drink. I find Applejack whiskey is a great treat among the ladies of Tennessee, so upon the whole, I will set my net for the smaller fish and let the big ones go. To tell the truth, Southern society in a moral and social point of view is *beneath* that of the Negro.

November 30

As the Captain was not released, I expect to remain here on duty for some time. The news from the Front is cheering indeed, and forms the theme for conversation. All kinds of rumors are afloat, and all kinds of conjectures made of the advance, but I content myself with the thought that the rebellion is played out. From two to five Rebel deserters come into our office every day to take the oath of allegiance, and they are a sorry looking lot. Ragged, dirty, and ashamed in their general appearance, I pity the poor devils and still I cannot help hating them.

How heartily they shake a Yank's hand and call him brother, after they have taken the oath. They are really disheartened and have given up the idea of establishing a southern confederacy. It is only surprising to see how willing they are to confess their guilt, and I believe they mean to do better in the future.

To sum up the labor for the month, I have issued 1,900 passes and written some promiscuous documents. Too, I have seen and talked with as many different characters, and I never saw such a variety before.

The white population is ignorant, habitually filthy and lazy. Many a one does not know what town he lives in. Eight of every ten cannot write their names, and some few do not know the day of the month or year that is passing, while there are a selected few that are intelligent, and they invariably thank the northern school, and teacher for their training.

December 2

The day dawned clear and beautiful, but cold, and for the first time this year I saw some snow. There was quite a severe storm in the night but by nine o'clock the bright sun had melted the last flake, and it was as pretty a day as I would wish to see.

During the day, Mrs. Rodgers (the wife of General Rodgers) sent word that I could come and board with her. I went to see her immediately, and, to be brief, she is as fine a lady as I would wish to see.

She introduced me to the whole family, consisting of a son and two daughters, and, really, they appeared like somebody. After a social chat, the old lady showed us through the house. The Rebels had destroyed the property for her to the amount of $4,000. Everything in her house that could be broken was in ruins. I then returned to the office, and, at four o'clock, went to supper, and it was a good meal. We had vegetables, sauces, roast beef, warm bread and butter, with white dishes to eat from. She boards us for our rations. It seems like home, and I am bound to stay there as long as I can.

December 5

Another pleasant and beautiful day has passed, and we have been blessed with the presence of the Paymaster. I received $43.50, and tonight I have listened to a string band playing their music and many a thought did it bring to my mind of the pleasant past. Besides, I have had all the cider and apples I wanted. In fact, I have enjoyed myself, only I am tired. The office has been crowded all day. The issuing of 150 passes has been the result of my labor for the day.

December 12

I have been employed as usual for the last week, only a little more so. In addition to the usual routine of labor, there has been the administering of oaths to Rebel deserters, who have been coming in by squads, and of whom there have been twenty-five to thirty per day.

They are a sorry looking lot. Some of them come in

bare headed and footed. They tell a pitiful story and re-
pent of their deeds, pledge their honors and lives to do
better in the future, and go on their way rejoicing. The
weather has been very disagreeable.

December 31

I have been very busy of late, and the consequence is
I have neglected my diary, but as this is the last day of
the year, I have resolved to write a summary of the past
few days and turn over a new leaf for the new year.

I have performed my duty at the desk faithfully,
being on duty constantly. The weather has been delightful, with only a shower occasionally, which only enabled
the boys to build their forts with more ease than otherwise.

The business of the office has been steadily increasing
and sums up thus: 225 oaths of allegiance to Rebel deserters, 3,000 passes and 1,000 permits to purchase
goods and groceries. Though the storm rages without
tonight and the searching blast sounds lonely enough, I
must say I have passed the evening very pleasantly with
General Rodgers and Lady. They are as kind hearted
and as intellectual people as I wish to meet. I listened
with interest to the General's story of his march up the
hill of science, his travels to foreign lands, his labors as a
statesman, and last but not least, his labors and suffering
in the present struggle.

He is old and gray-haired, but full of life and energy.
He has suffered so much at the hands of Rebels, that he
is the most desperate man I ever saw.

After returning from the General's, I have written to
F. and written the foregoing page. Thus closes the year
1863 with Ham.

1864

January 1

The weather has suddenly changed to bitter cold, so I have had but little to do. I have passed the day in writing. Though it has been no pleasant task, I enjoyed it in a measure, because I could perform my duty. I have often thought of one year ago today, when I was in Kentucky. The people could come and go at their leisure, purchase merchandise to suit themselves. Too, there seemed to be a little energy and prosperity left among the people, but today the scene is directly the opposite, and I am seated at a good desk and by a comfortable fire granting passes and privileges to the emaciated populace.

At evening I sat by the fire and nursed a toothache until late, when I took a stroll over town to prospect. Not a sound caught my ear until I passed an old rickety house, where I heard music and dancing.

I stopped at the door and entered the house to see

what was doing. Behold, I saw five ladies and well, I could not count the soldiers, in a little eight by ten room trying to dance. I remained a spectator while one set was dancing. When through, the ladies all drank freely of applejack, then taking a dip of snuff, formed on the floor again for a dance, and I left for quarters.

January 2

Today, as yesterday, is cold and bleak and if anything more lonely. The evening I have passed by a cheerful fire listening to the stories of a Rebel Captain (Cave). They were not only laughable, but truly characteristic of the southern people. The Captain is a Rebel deserter, had repented of his deeds, and now belongs to the federal army and is a useful man.

January 10

It is Sunday today, but no changed duty for me. Nothing outside the routine of other days to attract attention, and, as it has been rather cold for a few days, there have been but few in the office.

Late this evening Colonel Shafter brought the intelligence that our brigade had been assigned to the 13th Army Corps, which is now in Atlanta, Georgia.

January 11

I have busied myself as usual. The weather has changed to warm and is thawing quite fast.

Oh, yes, there was a company of the Corp d'Afrique came in town today under arms. I was quite surprised to see their efficiency in drill and soldierly appearance. It is evident they are to become a standing arm of the service.

January 12

The only excitement I have seen today and the only thing talked about upon the street is the Negro company of soldiers. It does me good to see the old master look upon his slave with fear when he gets a musket in his hands. After seeing the negro drill and go through the Manual of Arms, the master turns upon his heel, convinced for the first time in his life that the darky has an intellect, which can be cultivated and, when cultivated, is bound to shine.

January 13

It is again pleasant and summerlike. The snow-covered mountains contrast peculiarly with the barren and unfrozen valley. The pleasant weather invites the slothful Tennesseean out of burrow or hovel. Consequently, the office has been full to overflowing, and I have been unusually busy.

There was a little stir tonight among the soldiers, occasioned by the return of the negro company. It seems they were out in the country recruiting when a young man was heard to say he wished every negro soldier and officer would be captured before they could return to McMinnville, whereupon they arrested him and brought him to town. The assistant Provost Marshal, after scaring him pretty well, made him go before the negro company and (upon bended knees) ask their forgiveness. It caused a general shout.

January 15

Some of the scouts were fired upon and driven in today. One man was killed. He was wounded by the first fire and captured by the Bushwackers, who, to torture their captive, shot him seven times before he expired. The affray has created a spirit of revenge among the boys, and they have gone out in force to avenge the death of their comrade or lay waste the country. As usual, it has been a busy day with me.

EDITOR'S NOTE: *The term "Bushwackers" referred generally to the local guerilla forces who operated against occupying Union forces without any overall Confederate organization. They were especially active in Kentucky and Tennessee. As we have come to learn so well in later wars, the "slothful and ignorant" residents Ham processed daily in Provost Marshal's office duties, were often engaged at night in guerrilla operations against the Union troops.*

January 16

This has been a very pleasant and busy day. Our wagon train was attacked at Woodbury on it's way from Murfreesboro to this place. Two men are missing, and three mules killed, but the train got through safe.

January 22

The noted guerrilla. . .[unreadable] visited our picket line, but did no damage. Tonight he was reported to have killed two Union men in the country, which has since been learned to be a fact.

February 1

It has rained some today, but not enough to affect business. Upon the contrary, there appear to be more people in town than usual.

At night I was at a dancing party, and it was amusing to see the natives get off their breakdown. They could not dance a cotillion or fancy dance. They were mostly snuff dippers and I left the place in disgust at southern ladies.

February 4

The Captain has succeeded in getting me back to the company for a few days to do some writing for him. The company received twenty-six new recruits yesterday, and that creates some business for the company officers, and it really belongs to the Orderly, but they have piled it on me, and the Orderly Sergeant gets the pay for it. Such is a soldier's life.

February 11

The Captain laid out a day's work for me today, but

there was a grand rush at the office, and I was called back there.

During the day I saw two wenches fight, the most comic thing I have seen for a long time.

The excitement still continues about the raiders, and every effort is being made to meet them. Every man that can work upon the forts is at work.

A negro reported that the guards at the bridge were attacked by guerrillas this morning and taken. Company E was called for the reinforcements. The boys marched to the supposed scene of action and found the guards eating breakfast.

February 16

Notwithstanding our efforts to keep the people outside the lines, there have been countless numbers in town, and I have been unusually busy. My eyes are the worse for it.

The excitement about the raid has abated somewhat, but still there are preparations being made to meet the foe.

At dinner today I was introduced to Colonel Jarvis of the 13th Ohio and had a sociable time. I was alittle embarrassed, however, when the old lady asked me to carve the turkey, but I did it up in true soldier style.

February 18

It has been bitter cold today for this climate. The citizens complain a good deal about the cold, but the soldiers don't seem to mind it.

A forage train started out this morning. About noon they sent in for reinforcements, as they had encountered the Guerrilla Carter and his band. E Company was sent to their relief, and the boys went out with a shout at the prospect of a fight. At this hour (eleven o'clock) I propose to lay down my pen and rest.

February 19

I was relieved by request from duty at the Provost Marshal office this morning, and I feel like a bird set free. In the morning I went down to Wese's bakery and ate his fried cakes. In the afternoon I worked over the Company books, principally in the order book. I shall now have a better chance for life, and I will not be bored by the ignorant natives every day. The weather is very cool, especially the nights.

February 23

Today the 23rd Missouri Volunteer Infantry was ordered away, and we are once again left the sole occupants of the town. It is somewhat lonesome without them, but I expect it will come our turn to go next.

There has been a change at the Provost Marshal's office, and I have been there all day instructing the new clerk. The citizens are not satisfied with my leaving and are trying to get me back, but I do not crave the position. Tonight I moved back to the company, and it seems odd to be among so many. I have been used to still and quiet evenings, but now I shall have to get used to the noise of a company of men.

February 24

I have been writing muster rolls today. At evening
H.H. Pullman, W. Locke, and I walked to the western
part of town. We examined a redoubt commanding the
western entrance of town. It is irregularly built with
heavy banks, but it's inner works are not completed. It is
to contain one siege gun and block house. The latter is
nearly built. The work, when finished, will accomodate
about two hundred men. The day has been delightful.

February 26

I have noticed nothing today but my work, and have
completed my muster rolls and pay rolls, and now am
free from hard labor for a few days.

The evening I passed at my boarding place with Miss
Mary Rodgers. She sang and played upon the guitar for
me, and I had a good visit. I shall regret the day that we
are called to leave this place. I have really fallen in love
with the quiet and romantic place, and if I could think
as much of it's inhabitants, I should think of returning
to this place when the war is over.

The boys have completed the railroad bridge, and a
train starts for Tulahama tomorrow. I hope we will now
have the news daily, also the mail from home.

March 2

A part of the regiment was ordered to Pikeville today,
but they did not go. The Major went to Tulahama to
remonstrate against going at all, for there is hardly suf-

ficient force here to hold this place. The boys, however, are anxious to go merely for the change.

March 3

Five companies were called out to go to Pikeville. They went as far as Collins River, where they found the water so high that they could not ford, so they were obliged to return. They came into town about sundown, the boys were shouting, and the old Colonel was swearing.

March 4

Company E was again ordered to Nashville, Tennessee, this morning, and I concluded I wanted to go, so I borrowed a gun and went with the company, and tonight finds us at Woodbury, a little town of four hundred inhabitants situated in a little valley between the hills. It has been a thriving place, but, like all the towns in Tennessee, is deserted and torn down.

I traveled this same road the first of November, last, and it is useless to write it's principal features again. We are quartered in an old schoolhouse for the night. The orderly, L.A. Lamb, and I got a canteen of milk and made up our faces for a good supper, but when we commenced our meal, we found our milk was buttermilk.

EDITOR'S NOTE: *Ham was captured exactly a year previously only four or five miles from the spot in which he found himself in the next entry. It was a curious coincidence, and he remembers it well.*

March 5

At daylight this morning we were again upon the March. At Murfreesboro we drew rations and ate our dinner. At two o'clock we were again on the road.

The first scene after leaving town was Fortress Rosecranz, the next was the battle ground of Stone River. I have noted these same spots before, but we might pass over them a hundred times and find something new every time. Tonight we have quartered by the roadside. L.A. Lamb and I bought some milk that was sweet and made our supper upon bread and milk.

Often, today, I have thought of one year ago and wondered when we shall see another day such as that. It is not impossible for such a day to come, but I hope it never will. Yesterday was the 365th day since I carried a musket and it makes me lame and sore.

March 6

Early this morning we were again on the march. About two o'clock P.M. we arrived at Nashville, tired as I wish to be. After pitching our tents, Delos and I went up town and got a cup of coffee and some bread and butter, of which we made our supper, then returned to camp, built our bed and went to sleep. The road we have passed today has been a rough one and lined with army wagons.

The country is deserted and destitute except the idiot

asylum, which was preserved and is in full operation. It was as fine a farm as I ever saw. The orchard thereon was as good as could be asked for and very large, nearly a thousand trees.

March 7

Today I have been all over town. The narrow streets were filled with busy men and teams, and everything was lively, each seemingly striving to outdo his neighbor.

Among the crowd were loaded army wagons, each drawn by six mules, and the harsh and husky voices of their drivers sounded curiously and loudly enough to be heard above all else.

I had my picture taken and returned to camp. In the evening we went to the theater and had a very good entertainment by the Davenport Family. The City of Nashville I have described before, and it is only necessary to say here that is is the filthiest place I ever saw.

March 12

Today I have been appointed Color Guard and drew my musket. It is an old one and bears Rebel marks as belonging to a Mississippi Rebel regiment. It is quite a novelty and a much lighter gun than those of the other boys. In the afternoon, we were out drilling in our new capacity. There are nine of us that constitute the Color Guard, and we are an independent squad, all Non-commissioned Officers. Their names are as follows:

Sergeant W. M. Tyler,
Company C

Corporal G. B. Crawford,
Company A
Corporal R. Patterson,
Company B
Corporal H. Viven, Com-
pany D
Corporal H. A. Coe, Com-
pany E
Corporal N. Schott, Com-
pany F
Corporal I. Graham,
Company G
Corporal M. W. Simons,
Company H
Corporal Milo Hyde,
Company I
Corporal Charles Fuller,
Company K

March 13

This day has passed as Sundays usually do in camp. At four o'clock, P.M. the battalion went upon dress parade. There were two men from each company mounted this morning as scouts. When they were together upon their horses, they were desperate looking fellows, and, no doubt, will have some hard duties to perform.

March 22

Today it is almost winterlike. This morning the Colonel sent for me and put me in charge of the indigent people of the town and vicinity. It is a hard position to do justice to, but I am subordinate and must obey, therefore I will do the best I can.

Last night there was a skirmish upon the picket line. Our boys were up and watching for the Rebs. Our boys were not hurt, and what injuries the Rebs sustained is not known.

March 28

I was relieved at the Colonel's today, and I was heartily glad of it, for he is a cross old ————. Worst of all, when he tells a man to do a piece of work, he invariably does the work himself by telling his subordinate how to do it. I have made the return of C.C. and G. equipage for the company and a part of the ordinance return today, consequently have had but little time to play.

It has rained nearly all day. The snow has disappeared from the mountains, and it looks like spring upon all sides tonight, though the March winds are blowing a perfect hurricane.

EDITOR'S NOTE: *About the time of Ham's next entry, General U.S. Grant was appointed by President Lincoln as Supreme Commander of all Union forces.*

A Colonel G.F.R. Henderson wrote, years later, in his History of Stonewall Jackson *concerning the appointment of General Grant as Commander in Chief on this date:*

It is a significant fact that. . . . .for three years, the control of the Armies of the North remained in the hands of the Cabinet and the balance of successes lay with the Confederates. But in March, 1864, Lincoln abdicated his military functions in his [Grant's] favor. Then, for the first time, the enormous armies of the Union were man-uevered in harmonious combination and. . .full effect.

A very tired and a very frustrated President Abraham Lin-coln told General Grant on that day, "I neither ask nor desire to know anything of your plans. Take the responsibility and act, and call me for assistance."

It would be interesting to know if the "Henderson" Ham met and refers to in his diary is the same, or perhaps the father of the Colonel Henderson who wrote the History.

March 30

The day has been one peculiar to March, and I have kept within doors attending to company affairs. I made some reports, enlisted a negro as undercook for the company, and passed the remainder of the day in read-ing.

At evening, I chanced to be loitering about town and met a man named Henderson, who I found to be son of the Henderson who took so active a part with Daniel Boone in the settlement of Kentucky. He is an old man and rather intelligent in his rough way, and, having read the history of Boone, I had a good visit with the old man, and he told me many of the adventures of his boyhood on the frontier of Kentucky.

March 31

Long remembered will this day be as the day of our exit from Libby. The rain is falling today just as it did then, and if we were in Richmond the scene would be the same. We celebrated the eventful day with a meeting at the bakery. Wesley had a keg of beer, some cookies and some hot coffee, and it was midnight before we left.

I have passed the day in writing for the company. In the afternoon, cannon were heard in a southeasterly direction, probably at Shelbyville, but we are ignorant of the cause.

April 12

Another train went to Murfreesboro today freighted with contrabands. The weather is glorious and everyone seems to be enjoying the sunshine. Towards evening I had two teeth extracted.

April 13

My teeth continue to ache, and I had two more drawn today, and they are sore enough.

Today several of the officers and Misses of the town went to Bershebe Springs for a pleasure ride. The place is a summer resort for the upper tens of the south, and no doubt is a pretty place, situated as it is upon the summit of a mountain with nine springs to water the hilltop, and with the cool air and beautiful scenery it cannot fail to please the eyes.

There were a thousand and one remarks made by the boys as the company passed out the lines and I shall always remember some of them. One I will mention. It was about Miss Clift. She is very tall and was mounted upon a tall horse. Said one of the boys, "See that bean-pole on stilts?" Another said "Colonel, come back and get the colors for that woman to carry—she would make a good flagstaff !"

April 17

We had company inspection today. I wrote a letter. I was at the bakery to dinner and had a good one. Towards night a courier arrived from Murfreesboro with marching orders for the regiment to join the brigade at Tulahoma, and we shall have to go this time. The citizens murmer a good deal because we are going, but more because the 23rd Missouri volunteers are to relieve us.

April 19

About noon the Missouri regiment came in town. They were a sore footed set, and I could see how I would look in a few days, after marching as they had, tired and lame and hungry. Colonel Robinson assumes command of the post, and Colonel Gilbert is Oh! so mad. We are now awaiting orders. I have passed the time in preparations for the journey and writing letters.

April 21

Early this morning a long line of bayonets and blue coats could be seen upon parade. The next moment, our regiment could be seen marching through the streets of McMinnville for the last time.

Many a goodbye was said, and some I noticed shed

tears at our leaving. We have marched about nine miles
to the south. Upon one hand have been the proud peaks
of the Cumberland to be admired.

Tonight we are encamped upon Hickory Creek, and I
am for the first time tented in the dog kennels with
Wesley, Chris, and Hank P. We have had a gay time
putting it up.

Indeed, today has been a new era in military life for
me. Sergeant Tyler was sick, and he assigned the colors
to me. I wish some of those that saluted us this morning
were my friends from home. It would have done me
good to return the salute with the old flag.

April 22

I am writing the events of the day in my pup tent,
open at either end, with the soft breezes passing
through.

We have marched about twelve miles over the best soil
by far that I have seen in Tennessee. If the country had
been more thickly populated, I should have fancied I
was nearing my home in Michigan.

The greatest wonder is that this beautiful plain lies at
the foot of the mountains, and the mountains are a
gigantic piece of masonry for hundreds of feet above.

We passed a school in session today for the first time
in Rebeldom. The scholars were mostly ladies, some
older, some younger, and but a few small boys, while the
teacher was an old grey headed man of sixty summers
or more. When the regiment passed the schoolhouse,
they all flocked to the door. Our band played a national
air, while the boys gave such a yell as only soldiers can
utter. The young and the fair waved their handkerchiefs

Serving out rations

in response, but when the veteran teacher raised his hat and gave us a salute, the boys gave him three of the heartiest cheers I ever heard, and I could see the tears mount to the old man's eyes.

We made no halt, but passed on. At this moment we are camped near a little stream, clear and sparkling, having it's fountainhead in the mountains. My teeth ached all night, so I did not rest much and am tired enough tonight.

April 23

This day's march has been through fields, woods, and

over the hills, and the crookedest road man ever
traveled. Many times there was no road. We have
traveled about twelve miles along the western base of
Cedar Mountain. Mounting the hills, one could see the
Cumberland range, which is as magnificent as ever.

The scene around camp tonight is equally as beautiful.
The leaves of the trees are nearly at full size, and the
odor of many wild flowers is borne upon the warm and
gentle breeze.

The regiment stopped at a house to get water today.
The old lady came out and wished to see the American
flag, asserting that she had never seen it in her life, and
she had lived fifty long years. "This," said I, "is another
example of ignorance."

She was surprised to see a Yankee, but she could not
see the difference between the Yankee flag and the
Confederate flag. The boys are shouting all about camp
tonight. We have marched slowly, and the result is that
but few of the boys have straggled, and are all well.

April 24

Twelve o'clock finds us at Corwin Station and the end
of our march. The boys are well and noisier than ever.
We have marched but five miles today, but it has been
over the mountains, consequently toilsome. We have
camped upon a green lawn by a beautiful spring.

This station is at the great tunnel through the Cumberland Mountains of the Chattanooga railroad. It is
nearly surrounded by mountains. The scenery is fascinating to the transient observer, but I fear the fascina-
tion would not last long, as the country is too rough and
unfertile to become wealthy. We passed through this

place when prisoners, and the place looks natural enough. In our march today we were obliged to wade Elk River. It was waist deep. The boys stripped to the skin and were as merry as if they were swimming in the St. Joseph for a bath.

April 26

We have traveled fourteen miles of the roughest road I ever saw, such a one as only mules and soldiers can travel. Early in the morning we began to climb the western slope of the mountain. Gaining the top, we could look back and see the green valley and the little town we left in the morning, and it seemed scarcely a half mile to where we left camp. Looking still farther, we could see a half dozen towns and it was a beautiful sight.

We have passed three deserted houses. The rest of the road has been through the wilderness of heavy timber, which seems almost impassable. We camp in the open air tonight. I have carried my knapsack all day and am very tired.

April 27

Today we have marched but twelve miles. The fore part of the day we descended the mountains, and of all the hills I ever went down this is ahead. It was steep, and between a knapsack and the rocks we were somewhat stove up.

After tipping over a wagon and breaking one, we reached the base of the mountain and found ourselves in Anderson's Cove, which is a long and narrow valley, and upon either hand we have to look twice to see the tops of the mountains.

Everything is green in this valley. Garden sauce is quite plentiful. At noon we stopped at a spring, one of the largest and with as pure water as I ever saw. It emerges from the north base of the south mountain and abounds with fish.

At our camp, some five miles down the valley, this spring forms quite a river, where the boys have been swimming ever since we camped. The day has been as warm as July since we reached the valley, while the table land was cool, scarcely a leaf had started. I am seated upon the grass to write, with my coat and vest off. I sweat freely, so, laboring under the weight of a knapsack and the heat of a tropical sun, I have suffered considerably. Looking around me, I see a beautiful scene that I am incompetent to do justice with my pencil to. At my feet runs the clear and sparkling stream (Battle Creek), and a few rods beyond rise the lofty mountains.

April 28

We have marched about twelve miles today and I never stood a tramp better. About noon we arrived at Bridgeport, Alabama, and I noticed it is rightly named, for there is nothing there to designate the spot but the large bridges across the Tennessee River.

The town has been demolished and soldiers' shanties are built upon the ground, and Yankees inhabit them. We crossed the river upon a pontoon bridge, stayed but a little time, and again resumed our march.

We are upon the line of railroad that conveyed us to Richmond when we were prisoners, and it looks natural enough. I thought that we would stop by the way and do some duty, but I guess now we are going to the front. General R—'s division was camped at Bridgeport.

Thousands of troops are now going to the front, mostly V.K. They are all surprised to see our regiment, it is so large and noisy. The railroad is lined with trains loaded with army supplies and some soldiers, though most of the soldiers have to foot it from Nashville. While I have been writing, the above, four trains have passed. Tonight we are in the Tennessee Valley, and for miles in front of us can be seen Lookout Mountain.

April 29

We are encamped in an old Rebel earthwork at the northern base of Whiteside Mountain, the summit of which is cleared of timber, and the stars and stripes are floating from the forts that are built thereon.

Deserted rebel works appear on every hand, but they are poor excuses and, I am told, were taken easily. Whiteside Mountain, where the states of Georgia, Alabama and Tennessee join, alone commands the country, and it seems impossible to take, as it rises to nearly one thousand feet at an angle of forty-five degrees on all sides. The landmarks of the retreating enemy appear everywhere. There are carcasses of dead horses and mules, sometimes dozens together and as often as one every five rods, showing the cost of our efforts in this quarter.

Thousands of soldiers are buried by the way. A small spring of the best of water graces our camp tonight. The boys generally are well.

EDITOR'S NOTE: *When General Grant went east to assume command of all the Union Armies, he left General Sherman in command in Tennessee. Sherman's opposite in the Confederate armies facing him, General Johnston, had been faced for some months by rapidly deteriorating relations with President Jeff Davis.*

President Davis and General Bragg wanted him to assume the offensive in the west. They even offered him 75,000 new reinforcements if he would attack. Johnston said the plan was impractical and declined—he felt that it was better to let the Union armies advance and fight them far from their base and close to his own.

General Sherman, at the beginning of the Atlanta campaign, had an estimated 100,000 troops in the field.

April 30

We have marched about ten miles today through the rain, over hills and valleys ankle deep in mud. We started early and about ten o'clock we struck a railroad (I do not know it's name) at the base of Lookout Mountain.

We followed that until we passed the headquarters of General Hooker, General Butterfield, and the camps of three divisions. We camped upon a little sand knoll where we stayed long enough to rest, at least.

Our camp is at the northeast base of Lookout Mountain. From the view here, she rises at an angle of forty-five degrees until within about two hundred feet of the summit, where the rocks are perpendicular, so that it seems utterly impossible for any human force to storm it, but our forces did, and the point at which it was stormed would admit one company at a time. As we

"We struck a railroad at the base of Lookout Mountain."

passed the mountain it was raining, and the clouds completely enveloped it's summit. Chattanooga is but three miles from us to the Northeast. I am very tired.

EDITOR'S NOTE: *Lookout Mountain was captured by Union forces during the battle for Chattanooga some five months prior to Ham's entry above. Walter Geer, in his* Campaigns of the Civil War *gives this account of the events of 24th November, 1863:*

—there was a mist over the mountain, which later settled down into a dense fog. At eight o'clock Geary's division of the Twelfth Corps crossed Lookout Creek from Wauhatchie; it was joined on the left in the valley by Osterhaus's division of the Fifteenth Corps, and Cruft's division of the Fourth Corps.

—Aided by the fire of batteries on Moccasin Point, the Union forces pushed up the rocky slope, driving the Confederates from one position after another. By noon Hooker had possession of the Craven farm. Here, the Confederate brigade which had defended the slope was joined by the two brigades from the plateau, and a stand was made about 400 yards beyond the Craven house. This line was held until midnight, when the Confederates withdrew from the mountain. On account of fog and the exhaustion of his ammunition, Hooker halted his line and entrenched.

Late in the afternoon, a supply of ammunition was brought from Chattanooga—. Early the next morning —some men of the 8th Kentucky scaled the heights and hoisted the Stars and Stripes on the summit, where, at sunrise, the flag floated in full view of the Union and Confederate troops in the lines below.

May 2

There is a rumor in camp of a fight at the front. We are expecting to march every moment. The officers have been obliged to turn over their bell tents today and take pup tents. I imagine I can see some of them with their knapsacks on their backs laboring as I do.

May 3

Early the bugle sounded, and the brigade took up the line of march via the east and southern base of Lookout Mountain, leaving Chattanooga to the left in full view. Around the town are located camps and forts. Soon we came in sight of Missionary Ridge, which has nearly the same lines and proportions as Lookout, except it is not so high.

We arrived at Rossville about nine o'clock, where our

forces made the last bold stand upon their retreat from Chickamauga. The landmarks are as plain as they were the day of the battle. Every tree (the battle was in the woods) has a greater or less number of ball holes, and many a tree was cut entirely off by cannon balls and shells. The struggle seemed to be a short one. In brief, the road we have traveled today has been a vast battlefield.

We are encamped tonight near the field hospital of the battlefield of Chickamauga. Many trees eighteen inches in diameter were actually cut down with balls, while the underbrush is seemingly mowed down with musketry.

Old clothing and all kinds of war implements lay scattered upon the ground. The most interesting thing I saw was a rebel's letter to his brother, also a rebel. I tried to get possession of it but failed. The worst sight I saw was the dead that had been buried, particularly upon the ground the rebels occupied. They buried their own men decently, putting a board and inscription at the head of each, but the Union forces they covered so slightly that their hands, feet, and their skulls are now uncovered and exposed to the open air. They burned a great many and their bones are now lying with the ashes above the ground. *This I saw* and examined for myself. We found one that was buried with leaves of the forest. One whose feet and legs were unburied was actually petrified; but enough. I shall always remember the scene and pray God I may never see another such.

May 4

Resuming our march this morning, we passed over

the extreme right of the Chickamauga battle ground via
Lee's and Jordan's mills, where our division was encamped, and a pretty camp it was.

Lee and Gordon's mills. "A pretty camp it was."

From this place we threw out flankers and have been
treading contested ground all day. We have marched
cautiously through the wooded country, slightly uneven,
leaving Ringgold to our right. Tonight we are encamped
at the foot of Pigeon Ridge, and we are in line of battle.
Once more skirmishing is of daily occurrence in our
immediate front. Thousands of troops are encamped
about us, so it is evident we shall take part in the next
great battle which will be soon.

May 5

Our lines have been lengthened greatly today by the arrival of fresh troops. It is supposed we will March by tomorrow, as we could see the Rebs evacuating Tunnel Hill. Today is my birthday, and I am a wanderer.

May 6

This day we made a swift march to the right of our lines, and I am at a loss to tell our real position. We left camp in such a way that I was lost and have not yet learned the part we are performing.

We are but six miles from our position yesterday. Coming to a sudden halt, the boys began to throw up breastworks across an open field at a gap in the mountains, where we expected to bag some Rebs that our cavalry were drawing on, but at this hour, four o'clock, the work has ceased, and we have established camp for the night. It surprised me to see how quickly the boys made their preparation for a fight. They would cut down a tree and carry it bodily to the works, and the next moment the bank of earth would complete the work. In the short space of twenty minutes the line of works was complete, over three miles in extent, and in one half hour more the whole Corps would have been entrenched.

General Thomas and staff passed us today, and I saw him for the first time. The view I had of him was too brief to form an opinion of him, but his history is known too well to doubt his capacity, and I rejoice that he is with us. He has the confidence of the men in his command, and we shall follow him to victory I hope. We are now like a bird on the wing, uncertain where we go or when we go. Soon I expect to meet the foe.

May 7

At three o'clock the bugles sounded throughout the corps, and we had hardly time to make our coffee before the advance was sounded and entire Twentieth Corps was under motion. It was a grand sight to see thirty thousand men move at once. We marched at quick time passing to the left flank through a wooded country over hills and mountains until we gained about fifteen miles, halting at the foot of a hill, where we met the Cavalry troops of Kilpatrick's awaiting the infantry for the purpose of charging up the hill where it was supposed the Rebs were.

The 19th was in for it, and we gained the summit without a shot. We soon barricaded the hill with rails and logs. In twenty minutes we completed the line. Then we had supper of onions with meat, coffee and hardtack.

We are indebted to Christopher for foraging the onions and meat. Since supper I have had an opportunity to reconnoiter and find the Rebs are or are supposed to be posted upon the next hill in front of us. Our lines are extended, and if it is a possible thing old Joe will hem them in.

Tomorrow there is sure to be a fight or a foot race. I hope for the best and trust in Him who wields the destiny of all. In all we have marched about twenty miles. The boys generally threw away everything but their rations and ammunition. I am now tired and weary but well, and must rest.

Major-General George H. Thomas. "I rejoice that he is with us."

EDITOR'S NOTE: *Sherman's advance began on May 7th. Finding Confederate General Johnston's position too strong to attack in front, he sent McPherson on a flanking movement to the West to Snake Creek Gap, and ordered Thomas (Ham's commander) to support him by making a strong demonstration against Johnston's front.*

*General Sherman's armies, all committed at the time of Ham's entry to the capture of Atlanta, consisted of the Army of Tennessee under McPherson (25,000), the Army of the Cumberland, under Thomas (60,000), and the Army of Ohio, under Schofield (14,000).**

May 8

We have lain behind our breastworks all day awaiting an attack. About three o'clock the fight opened upon our right and left, but lightly. We gained Tunnel Hill and (as I understand our position) we occupy the summit of a circle of hills with the Rebs in the valley.

The skirmishing has not been very fierce, though it is somewhat loud. There are now 150,000 men lying as we are behind a row of muskets, and we shall see some work tomorrow. At least, it cannot be put off a great while longer. Something must be done soon. I have expected it all day.

Wood's brigade has been reconnoitering since nine o'clock intending to draw them on our center, but has not succeeded. Although I have heard the balls often before, I must confess I was a little unsteady, but I soon gained control of myself, and now I am afraid I should shoot if I could see a Rebel.

*Geer, *Campaigns of the Civil War,* pp. 371-72.

We are occupying a position between Tunnel Hill and Dalton. Our line is a letter C surrounding twelve thousand of the Rebs, and they are obliged to fight. We worked all night and were still at work in the morning upon the entrenchments, and God and the soldier only know how tired we are. We are living upon half rations. I find we marched over twenty miles yesterday, and our position today is only six or eight miles from the one we held upon the 1st Inst.

The boys are all eager for the strife and in good spirits, and with this large army and it's leaders, we will do something soon. I am waiting patiently the result of contemplated movements. The day has been very warm and the ground is dry and parched. In fact, a man sweats in his shirtsleeves.

I have thrown away knapsack and contents, save my rubber blanket, and shelter tent, and if it gets much warmer I shall leave them by the roadside. This making a pack mule out of a fellow is played out while warm weather lasts. The carrying of my load hurts me worse than sleeping upon the ground.

May 9

The balls opened up upon the extreme left this morning. I supposed it to be General Howard's forces. The roar of the cannon has been loud and constant, and the roar of musketry has been inceasing. I have been lying in the shade all morning listening to the fray, expecting every moment the tide of battle will sweep this way. Our rest here has been a Godsend for us, for we were overheated and overmarched in the heat of a southern sun.

At this hour, twelve o'clock, the battle still rages upon

our left, the commotion and roar of which I am unable
to describe. Only those who are can understand it, so I
shall put up my diary, lie down upon my blanket and
await with suspense the time for the 19th to take part. .
At eight o'clock in the evening the battle still rages and
the tide is rolling to and fro. We receive no tidings but
the little we see and hear, We can see but two siege
guns, and they have been firing upon Buzzard's Roost
all day.

The musketry and light artillery is just audible beyond
the hills, and at times the strife seems at an end, then
again it is resumed louder than before. The boys have
become tired of hearing the strife and are anxious to
lend a helping hand. Colonel Coburn arrived and took
command of the brigade. Again the boys welcomed him
with a shout, although it was against orders to make any
noise in camp. The 33rd Indiana is with him.

May 10

We lay upon our arms until two o'clock, when we received marching orders to go to a hidden pass in the
Johns Mountains and hold the Rebs in check there. Sunrise found us in our position, and now the command is
"resting in place".

The expedition consisted of the 20th Connecticut
regiment and the 19th Michigan. The fight has not
opened this morning. The fight commenced again about
nine o'clock and has raged at intervals all day. Although
the Rebs are in full sight upon the summit of the mountain, and the boys have passed many a saucy word with
them, there have been but few shots fired upon our
side, wounding a Sergeant of Company I badly. The

skirmishers advanced about half way up the mountain where they met the Rebel picket. We have been lying in line of battle all day at the foot of the mountain.

May 11

Last night we retreated to a little hill in our rear for a safer resting place. The dusk of evening covered our movements. We had hardly time to pitch our tents before a thunder shower greeted us, and the rain descended in torrents. The Captain and Lieutenant Coblentz bivouacked with us in our tent. We were drenching wet and somewhat crowded and had a hearty laugh and joke in discussing the merits of our pup tents. When the rain descended so fast, the strife ceased, only to be renewed this morning. Directly in front of us and not a half mile distant the sharp notes of musketry are heard, and it seems as though they are storming the Rebel heights.

Various rumors are afloat, but none that can be relied upon. As yet, the 19th has not been engaged, close as we are to the Rebel lines. At this hour (noon) we are in line and ready to march and will again join our lines upon the right.

We have made a forced march of about twelve miles, joining McFerron's Corps upon the extreme right. Passing the 1st and 2nd divisions at Dug Gap, the 3rd Division is encamped in Snake Creek Gap. It is a deep gorge between two ranges of mountains. Deep and narrow, it is a most dismal place.

Though the bugle and drums sound throughout the valley, and the commotion and excitement are great, we are now beyond the hearing of the strife at Buzzard's

Roost, but it will not be long before we have a fight here. The general assault must be made soon, and we shall have to charge John's Mountains, which will be a greater task than it was to scale Lookout. The time passes quickly, but strangely enough for one who is alone.

May 12

We moved to the right today, taking position behind the 15th Army Corps, went into camp and there remained in line of battle. It is evident now that we are coming closer to the Rebs.

May 13

Again we moved to the right, passing the 15th and 16th Army Corps. We are now in line of battle by battalion closed in mass by division, and it is impossible to escape the strife longer. There are skirmishers in front exchanging an occasional shot. At ten o'clock we again moved to the right flank, gaining a position opposite to the one we held the last two or three days and in the rear of the Rebel's stronghold (Buzzard's Roost and Dalton).

The firing commenced about four o'clock, and it has been an incessant roar ever since. The boys went in with a yell that sounded above the din of battle, taking three heavy guns. Thus far our division has not been engaged, but we expect to every moment.

It is now sundown and the musketry is still firing. We are now lying in line of battle by division closed to mass, and while I sit here writing what a scene is presented!

In front is the roar and din of battle. The boys about
me are talking upon many subjects, and invariably they
are making light of the strife before us, and I never saw
the boys cooler or more steady.

Directly in our rear, regiment after regiment is passing double quick to their relative positions. To be brief,
it is a wilderness of bayonets and sabers where we are
now resting. Still farther in the rear are the ambulances
carrying off the wounded. What part we shall be called
upon to perform God only knows. Action is inevitable,
and God protect the right.

EDITOR'S NOTE: *The Confederates withdrew to Resaca (five
miles from the Union Lines) and were reinforced there on May
13.*

*On the morning of the 14th Sherman's advance was re-
newed. On the night of the 15th, the Confederates were forced
to abandon Resaca and begin a retreat to Adairsville some ten
miles nearer Atlanta. Sherman ordered full pursuit.*

May 14

The battle opened early upon the left, more terrific
than before. The earth is ajar with concussion. The
strife has been the heaviest directly in front of us. Until
this hour (four o'clock) the battle rages upon the extreme left. Millions only will count the shots that have
been fired today, and the victims will be counted by
thousands.

Fortune has favored us in that we are being held in
reserve thus far today, but our turn must come. It is
now almost dark, and the battle still rages. The roar is as

incessant as it was at noon. I know nothing of the battle or how it is waging only that I hear. That is that our forces have advanced to the Rebel position, and thus far hold the battle ground. I have heard and met the storm of battle before, but never so severe and long as today.

We were only too lucky to escape the storm, but the storm is not yet over, and we cannot lie in reserve through the whole of this great battle. The 14th and 15th Army Corps were repulsed upon the extreme right today, but at all other points our forces were successful.

May 15

Today we were led into the strife, and I hope I can forget the events of the day. By the guidance of Him who protects us all, I was saved to tell the tale.

Early in the morning we were moved to the left of our lines to support General Howard. At eleven o'clock we were ordered to charge the Rebel works upon the heights. The boys charged over a whole division that lay upon the ground in front of us and gained the first hill, the Rebs fleeing as we advanced.

Our success was such as to inspire the boys with double courage, and they could not be halted, but on they went to the next hill, capturing a fort and four splendid cannon and lay under the Rebel breastworks all day to hold the fort.

A good many of the boys were picked off by sharpshooters. The regiment lost one hundred one in all. Although our regiment was broken and in disorder, they charged like tigers. I was with the guard of colors. There were ten of us when we charged, and only three came off the field. I brought the old flag off the field, torn and riddled with balls. The boys cheered the rags when I brought them off, and we had a grand greeting.

The loss in Company E was heavy, nine wounded and three killed, one of whom was W. Mugg, and three missing. There are hundreds of instances that I would like to record, but I shall remember them only too well. It enough to say that we sustained a galling fire, and the boys behaved nobly, broken as they were.

May 16

The fight was kept up until twelve o'clock last night, and what a scene! I cannot describe it.

At six o'clock the cannon pealed forth their notes of thunder, sending the deadly shell among the Rebs, and the musketry was one continual salvo. The balls flew thick as rain, but wild and far above us, but all at once the demon yell rose above the din of battle, and the next order was "Charge Bayonets", clear and distinct. The next moment we had possession of the Rebel works, and the battle was over.

Under this fire, Colonel Coburn took off the four cannon we captured during the day. A shout accompanied our success.

Early in the morning we marched through the Rebel works, marching all day and part of the night. Crossing the Coosawacha River, upon a ferry, we camped for the remainder of the night.

I am tired and almost worn out, but I am well and the boys are in fine spirits. Our division captured a Rebel commissary on the march today, and they made a clean sweep of everything. We passed hundreds of dead Rebs and horses today, and everything in the shape of the

ammunition of war was lying along the road, showing a
hasty retreat of the Johnnies, and we are pushing them
hard and fast.

May 17

We have marched all day in pursuit of the Rebel
Army. We come upon a squad of them, occasionally,
and capture them, but their main army is in full retreat,
and our victorious columns are pursuing.

We captured a Rebel train of about four hundred
wagons today and burned them, besides capturing a
good many prisoners. Our division is upon the extreme
left and are the flankers, so we have to march about
three times as far as is necessary. The boys are tired and
worn out, but generally well. As for myself, I am too
near tired out to stand the running fight much longer.
A good many of the boys have fallen out by the roadside
today.

May 18

Again today we have chased the Rebs, marching about
twenty-five miles. We came upon them at sundown, and
the cavalry had quite a skirmish, capturing some prisoners and driving the Rebs like chaff before the wind.
Other columns to our right captured a number of prisoners and a battery of Rebs.

We were marched beyond reason today, and hun-
dreds of the boys were tired out and lay by the roadside.
I kept up but I am the tiredest man that ever lived.
When will this running fight ever cease? Hundreds of

men are suffering more from marching than from fighting. God speed the time when this strife will cease.

For the last three days we have passed through some beautiful country, rolling and wooded, though not very well cultivated. Save now and then a plantation, every place is generally deserted, especially by the male inhabitants, and the boys have gathered garden sauce at every house. Some of the gardens were good and vegetables nearly full grown.

May 19

Today the Rebs were still in front of us, and action soon became general. It has been a fight and a race all day. The sun was very hot, and the men suffered greatly therefrom. We were marched and countermarched until we were tired out, then were ordered to charge in line of battle. The boys did it in gallant style, but many dropped by the way, overheated and unable to go any farther. For miles we went through the brush and tanglewood until we gained the summit of a little hill.

We were ordered to support a battery, but the Rebs soon silenced our battery, and again we were ordered to charge the town of Cassville.

They did it in the same gallant style. With some resistance, we pushed on and gained a complete victory. Some of our boys were killed and wounded. One from our company and one from Company I fell by the side of the colors.

The old 19th Flag was the first to enter the town with the regiment. Our company suffered greatly from fatigue, many dropping in the ranks. We started this morning with forty men, and after the capture of the town we could stack but sixteen guns. The brigade was hardly as large as the 19th Regiment was two weeks ago.

As for myself, I stood the hardship well, but such marching and charging will soon use me up; but we must soon go, so I must rest for the night.

EDITOR'S NOTE: *On the 19th, Confederate General Johnston announced his intention of making a stand at Cassville in a stirring address to his troops.*

When, however, General Sherman partly turned the East flank of the Confederate line (in Ham's sector) Johnston's Generals Polk and Hood persuaded him against accepting battle there and the Confederate armies retreated through Cartersville to positions just south of the Etowah River. The center of the Union Armies was now 25 miles from Atlanta.

May 20

Today we have retired to the rear for rest, and we are the happiest lot of fellows in Christendom. There is no one to whom rest is so sweet as the soldier who has been relieved from a battlefield of fifteen days. Were all of our boys here to mingle with us we would feel still better, but alas, some are gone to return no more, and some are suffering from wounds, and our ranks are thin and emaciated.

Today, the company stacks but thirty-nine guns, and when we left McMinnville, the company stacked sixty-five guns. Such are the destructions of war.

We are now encamped, about three miles in the rear of the town of Cassville that we captured last night. It is in a shady woodland, and we have improved the time by resting. The town (Cassville) is the prettiest I have seen in the South. The streets are wide and well shaded with ornamental trees and shrubs. The buildings are mostly frame, and new. The courthouse is a nice brick structure and has as pretty a yard as I wish to see.

As we advanced last night, the inhabitants fled, and the boys helped themselves to tobacco, cigars, molasses, sugar, hats, caps, and, in fact everything they wanted, but private houses were not molested, and this morning the women and children began to come out of the cellars and hiding places, so the town assumed the air of civilization. I wrote two letters since the battle, but they were poor excuses.

May 21

Bare headed and barefooted, we have been lying about camp resting, each in his own way, and all appear to be enjoying and improving the time. I have written a letter, then copied some resolutions for Lieutenant Easton upon the death of Captain Calmer of Company I, 19th Regiment Volunteers, who was killed at Resaca in the battle of Sunday. Towards night Willard and George Rich and Byron Dunn of the 74th Indiana and Charles Peasley came to see me, and we had quite a visit. The day has been a bright and lovely one, peculiar only to the sunny south. The hours pass swiftly in this large army, but we have hardly waked from the strife we have just passed.

May 22

We have passed the time in camp, and we have rested

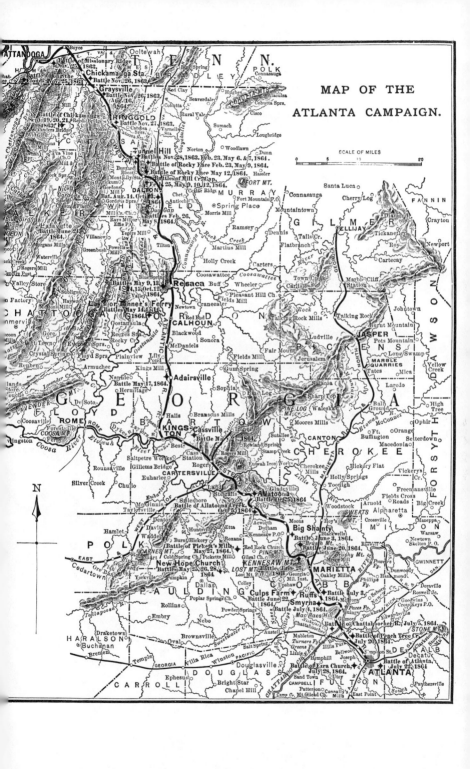

MAP OF THE

ATLANTA CAMPAIGN.

SCALE OF MILES

"Captain Calmer . . .was killed at Resaca in the battle of Sunday."

so long the boys begin to feel like themselves once more, though we miss those that are sick and wounded. Sergeant Lock went to the rear last night because of

wounds. We have received marching orders for tomorrow with twenty days rations, and I wish I knew where
we are going to.

I expect that time will bring about the events fast
enough. I was appointed Sergeant today, vice William
Smith, deceased, and am now Acting Orderly. I dread
the coming march, but such is the fortune of a soldier.

EDITOR'S NOTE: *After three days of rest, Sherman advanced to
Johnston's new position at Allatoona Pass. He deployed three
cavalry divisions on the flanks and rear of his armies, and the
fourth cleared the front for the Union infantry attack. Twenty
days' supplies were carried in the wagons: some 2,000 wagons
and 12,000 animals.*

At four o'clock this morning we started upon the contemplated march, and we have had a sorry old day of it.
It has been very warm and sultry. We marched in two
lines to the right, coming to the river about noon. Here
I expected our crossing would be disputed by the Rebs,
as it was.

The 4th and 14th Corps were fighting for the crossing
of the river. We were marched unreasonably, and hundreds of the boys fell out. Some of them were sunstruck.
H.H. Pullman gave out today, and we all came very near
it, but I kept my place at the head of the company. We
crossed, however, and were sent upon picket immediately.

May 24

We have been relieved from picket and now are lying
in the shade while other troops are reconnoitering.

We have stood the brunt of the brigade thus far, and our Major has the promise of remaining off duty for a time. I am glad of it, for we need it sorely. Our company only numbers thirty-seven men this morning out of seventy-two that we started with from McMinnville.

The cavalry skirmished in front of us some, but we were in camp before sundown, tired and sore. A good many of the boys fell out. It has been very warm. Before noon, we passed over some beautiful country. It has been a cotton growing section, but now hundreds of acres are sown to corn and wheat, and the growing crop looks well, wheat headed and in bloom. Fruit is plentiful and greatly advanced.

This afternoon we passed through a hilly country, then climbed the Altoona Mountains, and it seemed quite natural to get among the hills. Now I must quit my writing and attend to the wants of the company.

May 25

Again today we have marched hard and fast upon the summit of the Altoona Mountains, taking a southeasterly direction. We came upon the enemy at four o'clock P.M. and engaged them immediately. They were in their breastworks and fought hard.

Our loss was heavy. Our regiment was under fire about two hours, and the balls flew in a perfect shower, though but comparatively few shots took effect. Darkness ended the strife, and a severe storm soon surrounded us with darkness. We lay upon the line of battle until about one o'clock, when we were relieved by another regiment and went to the rear, tired and hungry.

We have had no rations today, and the boys murmur some, but have stood up nobly, sustaining the good reputation they have gained before, It is generally supposed we have quite a force to contend with here, and we expect a severe contest. The 20th Corps seems to be alone today in the fight, but other troops are coming up. God protect the right, and when the strife is ended, may it be in accordance with His will. Sherman, Hooker and Schofield are with us, and our destiny lies in their hands or management and in our labor.

May 26

Night is now coming on, and the clouds threaten a storm. I was awakened by the Lieutenant this morning, and the first sound that greeted my ears was the sharp crack of the musket upon the skirmish line. There has been a heavy skirmish kept up all day and the building of breastworks has gone on under their fire, but no general engagement has been brought on, though there is time enough yet tonight for a battle.

We are lying within three hundred yards of the Rebel works, and have been expecting to advance all day, but maneuvering seems to be upon the other parts of the line.

I am heartily glad of the rest that has been given us today, for we needed it greatly. The Rebels are going to make a desperate effort at this place, and the storm must break forth in all it's fury ere long. I look for it by tomorrow's sun. We have lost one man killed upon the skirmish line today. There has been no report made of the loss in last night's battle. It is enough to know that it was severe for the time we were engaged.

The day has been clear and pleasant, and I have slept soundly a part of the time. If I can rest tonight, I shall be much recruited. Last night we lay upon the battle ground, where the groans of the wounded and dying sounded dolefully, mingled with the storm of the heavens. I hope and pray for a better resting place tonight.

May 27

The battle opened again today upon the left, more fiercely than yesterday, but in front of us there was nothing engaged but the skirmishers. We have guarded a regiment in front of us that has been building breastworks. Some few of our boys were hit by stray shots, but few were hurt. They have all worked hard with the axe, pick and shovel. Tonight we have two lines of works now in front of us, and we are pretty well prepared for a fight. It is supposed the Rebs have their artillery massed in front of us, and I hope it will not be our duty to charge them. Night closes the scene. I have been somewhat busy with the company and tired enough to sleep if I can have that privilege.

May 29

The same as yesterday we have lain behind the works and listened to the balls whistling over us. One was killed from Company C.

The boys have been lying in the dirt so much and marched so long that they are dirty and ragged. We have a prospect of being relieved tonight.

May 30

We had hardly laid down last night when we were aroused by the roar of battle upon our left. Almost at the same instant the battle opened upon our right. The Rebs made the attack upon us and were handsomely repulsed. The fight was of short duration, but fierce.

All night the Rebs were moving troops in front of us and fortifying. Various opinions are entertained as to the cause of the attack. Some think it was a blind. All is quiet this morning except upon the skirmish line, where an irregular fire kept up all night.

The morning is clear and lovely, and it is going to be a warm day. About ten o'clock we were relieved and sent into the second line for rest. We cleaned up some, but, not having any soap, it was a kind of dirty wash.

At night we were counting upon a good night's rest, but about eight o'clock we were ordered to relieve a brigade to the left of our position, and we are now lying in the front line of works and upon the skirmish line. The brigade is suffering greatly from exposure and such constant duty, but such is the fate of a soldier.

May 31

Again today we have lain under the breastworks, rolling in the sand, and sweating under the effects of a southern sun. They have kept up a constant fire upon the skirmish line, and occasionally a cannon boomed forth its notes of thunder.

Again tonight brings quiet, and we are still lying down with belts upon us and guns in our hands, while we await patiently for the coming events.

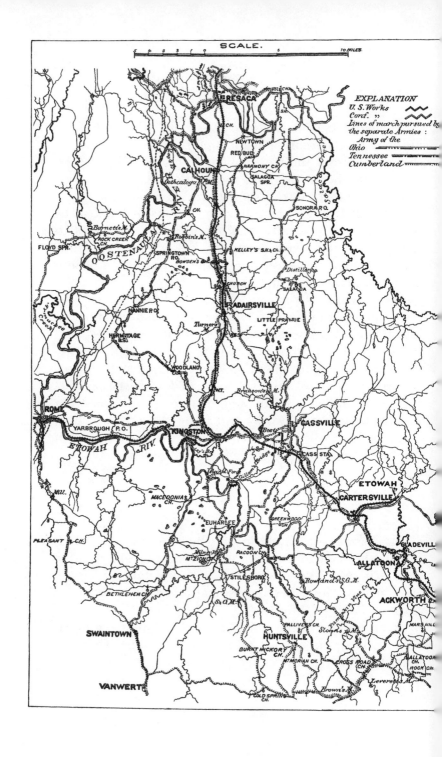

June 1

The rising sun found us in the same position. I have busied myself with the company, drawing rations, etc.

About two o'clock we were relieved by the 15th Corps and moved about five miles to the left of our lines, where we encamped for the night. We built our beds of leaves upon the hillside and took off our clothes to sleep for the first time in two long weeks, and never was sleep more sweet or reviving than last night's was to me.

Our stay here is but momentary. Although our progress is slow, we can only be patient. My expectations and speculations are many, and I am watching and praying for the end. I wish I could hear from home. The time seems so long.

June 2

We laid on our arms tonight in the mud and water, and it was a sorry old night. The boys have been without rations all day, and there has been a good deal of murmuring. Too, it has rained all day, and it is with difficulty that we have kept our guns and ammunition dry.

About noon Lieutenant Coblentz was taken sick and went to the hospital, which leaves me in command of the company. I carelessly forgot to get the company papers of the Lieutenant and had to go three miles to the rear after them. I found the Lieutenant somewhat better and hope he will be up soon, for being Captain, Lieutenant and Orderly of a company is more than I should like to shoulder.

While I was gone to the hospital, the regiment moved to the left, leaving me behind, but fortunately I found the Quartermaster, who was going to the regiment with rations and had no trouble to find them.

Arriving at the regiment, I drew rations for the company and divided them in the dark, the rain pouring down in floods. Chris and Hank had the tent up and some rails laid down to keep us out of the mud and water. The command is camped about two miles from our position last night, with regimental front closed in mass.

The boys stand around wet to the skin and in mud half knee deep. They look as though they had lost their last friend. These are sorry old times. We get no information of our own progress here, but are constantly moving or fighting. The results we must wait for patiently until a full report is made, and then we generally get it from home, but worst of all, we get no news from home, and I pray daily for a letter.

June 4

Again today we have remained in camp until four o'clock, when we moved directly to the front of our camp about eighty rods and took a position behind the line of breastworks, which the 23rd Corps had just left to advance upon the Rebs.

They had quite a heavy skirmish with them while we were taking our position, but all is quiet now, save an occasional shot; upon the right there has been some heavy firing, but we have no tidings from that quarter. It seems we are driving the Rebels slowly towards the railroad on the left, as we have possession of the Rebel works on our right. Our commanders seem to be satisfied with the progress of the army, and I must be. It has rained at intervals all day.

EDITOR'S NOTE: *General Johnston's confederate armies were indeed retreating slowly toward Atlanta, as Ham has surmised. Union General Sherman's style did not include frontal assaults against heavy confederate concentrations. His principle purpose during this period was to destroy as many of the Rebel forces as possible. The advance on Atlanta was brutal for both sides. The whole country was a terrible quagmire of mud, and this greatly hampered movements and supply operations. It was to rain continously until June 27, and the mud and the dense forest made any artillery help for the infantry nearly impossible, so the advance on Atlanta until the last of June became a battle of Infantry in unshaken earthworks. The toll on both sides in illness from the exposure to the elements was terrible. But, at the end of the campaign, Sherman's tactics as opposed to Grant's frontal assault phobia in his campaign on the eastern front against Lee showed the difference:*

*With almost exactly the same number of troops involved in the campaigns on both sides and in both campaigns (100,000 Union, 60,000 Confederate) Grant's casualties were over 50,000, while Sherman had lost less than 30,000. Both campaigns were made in very difficult country.**

June 5

Today has been all peace and quiet. We remained in camp, where we have cleaned up. Most of the boys went to church, or rather to hear a sermon from a Chaplain of another regiment. I was too busy to go. Having inspection and providing for the wants of the company occupied all my time, except a few moments, which I devoted to my friends at home.

We have poor encouragement to write home, for mail

---

*Geer, *Campaigns of the Civil War* (New York, 1926), pp. 381-82.

is so irregular. It has been one week today since the mail came to the army. Various rumors are afloat tonight as regards our progress here. Though I cannot believe all I hear, I do believe we are coming out ahead, or we would not be lying here idle.

June 6

This day has been one of toil and hardship, more so than any I have experienced. It has been warm and sultry, with a shower at intervals. Early in the morning we were ordered on the march, and before sunrise we were moving slowly to the left, toiling over muddy hills and open fields until about noon, when we suddenly came upon the Rebs. We were immediately thrown forward in single line of battle (our force consisted only of the 20th Corps) and, being without support, we halted and began to fortify our position. The boys worked with a will, and the works progressed rapidly, so that within an hour from the time we commenced, we were secure from an attack, but we labored hard all the afternoon to complete the works, which are quite formidable. The boys are the tiredest I ever saw them. I can speak for myself at least, but I am not yet done working. I must go and draw rations for the boys, for they are hungry and almost out of rations. I am too tired to work tonight, but I suppose this is the disadvantage of being commander of a company.

June 7

Last night I waited and watched for our rations until

two o'clock, then laid down to rest, and today we have been lying behind our works in comparative quiet. The boys have brought in a few of the Johnnies, but most of them were willing prisoners. I do not feel any the best today, but it is owing to the labor I performed yesterday, and a good night's rest with that that we have had today will make me all right again. Although this has been a rainy and cloudy day, it has been the gladdest one of the campaign for me, for I received two letters from home, which is a rare treat. I said this has been a day of rest. We have had to scour our rusty muskets and go on general inspection, which occupied most of our time. I had to command the company on inspection. I presume I was somewhat awkward, but all went off well, except one man. They complained of his musket a good deal. I find it is a hard task to command a company of men. One needs more patience than a schoolmaster and a good deal more energy and decision.

June 8

Today we have lain behind our works enjoying the shade, and it has been a pleasant day, pleasant because we have had an opportunity to wash our clothes and persons and rest in the cool shade of the forest trees. It has not been so pleasant for me, however, for I have been very busy. Yet it did me good and gave me pleasure to see the boys enjoy themselves. Lieutenant Coblentz returned today and has taken command of the company, which relieves me greatly, and yet I have enough to do, too. I have gone into a mess with the Lieutenant, and we have a man to cook for us, so that helps me some. We have no reports from the parts of the line, but, as we have heard no firing, it is generally supposed all is quiet. Our pickets were advanced to-night, and a general advance is ordered for tomorrow.

June 9

We were ordered to advance at an early hour this morning, but the order was countermanded, and we have been in camp again all day. Although I have been busy, the time passes slowly. In fact, time has been a drag today. I have had company inspection, which occupied some time, and the remainder of the day has been devoted to the interest of the company and in writing letters home. A reconnaissance of cavalry was sent out today in front of us, and they had quite a skirmish. I have not learned the results. This morning some of our boys had quite a time exchanging papers with the Rebs, and they seemed to have a good time between themselves. It commenced by our boys asking the Rebs to exchange papers, when both parties started with a paper waving over their heads and without arms. The Rebs were eager to exchange tobacco for coffee. Among other agreements was one to discontinue firing upon pickets.

June 10

This morning we were packed and ready to march by sunrise, but were ordered to await orders. It has rained nearly all day, so we were obliged to sit around all day with our rubbers over us, and then we could not keep dry, but about four o'clock we were notified that we would remain upon our old camp ground for another night, so the boys pitched tents and again are comfortable, except for rations. They are slim, and the boys are growling like hungry men will. There seems to be but little done along the line, though the corps have been moving in all directions, and they are now in advance of our lines. Some artillery firing has been heard, but with what result no one knows. All is quiet again tonight.

EDITOR'S NOTE: *On the day the Confederates had been forced to retreat to just north of Marietta, Georgia, Confederate Generals Johnston, Polk, and Hardee were reconnoitring on Pine Mountain in front of the Union center when General Polk was struck by a shell from a Union battery and killed instantly.*

June 11

The morning is a gloomy one, being cloudy overhead and muddy underfoot, and the more gloomy and disagreeable from want of rations. We have not suffered before for something to eat, but the boys have had nothing to eat this morning and but little last night. The rations are up with us, and I have done all I could to get them. The boys complain bitterly, but there is no redress. We are ordered to march at eight o'clock this morning, and now are waiting for the tedious and lonesome time to pass for action. All day it has rained, and all day have we waited in breathless suspense for the order to march, but tonight finds us in the same camp, with a prospect of sleeping upon the same spot we did last night. The boys have been without rations all day, and the murmuring is pretty loud. All I have been able to get for them was a small piece of beef. The 4th, 23rd, 14th, and 17th

Army Corps have been massing all day in front of us, but have not engaged the enemy other than by skirmish. Artillery has been throwing shell into the Rebel works all the afternoon, but they do not seem to get a reply. The object, I believe, was to shell them off a hill they are holding. There is something about artillery firing that I do not understand. The Rebels seldom fire their cannon except when they can use grape and canister. Upon inquiry, I learn that our gunners seldom fail to dismount their guns when they can get their range, which partially accounts for their silence. Another is that our forces seldom fail to silence their batteries with sharpshooters when they open upon us. The day closes gloomy and cloudy.

June 12

I have not felt very well today, though I have worked hard all day in the rain, drawing rations and clothing. It has rained steadily all day and is raining yet tonight. We have lain about in the weather until we are wet and muddy. There is not much doing here in the army, in fact, the army is stuck in the mud. There is some firing upon the skirmish line and some artillery firing, but no advance of our lines. We received mail today, and I was made the recipient of one only, but that was a welcome one.

June 13

It is still raining, and we are wet to the skin. I am almost sick or discouraged on account of it. We have raised our tent and built our bunk off the ground, so let it rain. Towards night the storm slackened apace, and we have now a prospect of a clear night once more. There has been a detail of twenty men made from the company for a train guard. There are a hundred and fifty from the regiment. It leaves but few in camp, so I hope I shall not have so much to do for a few days. There has been no advance made today, but the same as yesterday there has been artillery firing and some musketry, but no general engagement. Our line has been advanced a few rods.

June 14

The sun made its appearance in the east this morning, and for once we have had a clear day. We lay in camp all day, thus having a chance to wash and clean up, and I notice quite an improvement in the boys this evening. Their guns glisten in the evening sun, and their clothes (comparatively speaking) look as if they had come from the wash but an hour ago. I have busied myself with company business and writing letters. The army has been a little more in earnest today, keeping up a heavy skirmish fire and more artillery fire than I have heard since the fight at Resaca. The fighting has been in the 23rd Army Corps upon our left. We have been shelling the Rebs off the hills in front of us. A regiment of artillery fired by volley in the afternoon, and it was the loudest tumult I ever heard.

June 15

This forenoon we remained in camp as usual, but about noon, we were ordered to strike tents, and ere many moments had passed the 20th Corps was in motion. Passing a little to the right, we moved for the front. On we pressed, passing the 23rd Corps works, which they had evacuated. Coming upon the Rebel works, which were also evacuated, we made a halt, but only for reconnaissance. The 1st Brigade of our division was the scouting party. They found the enemy strongly posted upon an opposite hill. Halting upon the base of the hill, they waited for reinforcements and then made the attack. It was dreadful for a few hours. Many a poor fellow fell, and we gained nothing but a little ground. The 19th lost our Major (Griffin) in this onset. He died as nobly and bravely as he has ever shown himself upon the field of battle. The strife has been in a thick woodland, as usual. Today the fire has been very heavy, and we now lie so close to the Rebel works that I can hear every word of command that is given by them, and at this hour they are raining grape, canister and shell upon us. The sun set clear and bright, too lovely for the scenes about us, but such are the horrors of war. Will God forgive men for such work is a question I often ask myself, but I receive a silent reply and utter my own prayers for the safety of my poor soul and my country. I have seen hundreds of incidents today that I should like to mention, but my memory is too keen to forget all I see, and should I survive this strife I will write them when I have more paper and more leisure. I should like to be a newspaper correspondent now, so I could write all I should like to.

June 16

Late in the night we moved a little to the left and took

a position in the brigade, and under heavy skirmish fire the work of fortifying commenced. Although the boys were tired and careworn, they worked manfully until the works were done, but the dawn of morn revealed the fact that our works were in such a shape that the Rebels had an enfilading fire upon us, and we were in a critical position until we could build enfilades, and then we were obliged to lie close under the works. The ground is a little descending towards the Rebel works, so that the Rebels have all the opportunity of picking off our men. Here I am sorry to record the news of H. H. Pullman being wounded, W. M. Culver wounded and C. F. Crippin killed, making a loss of three out of the thirteen men of Company E that went into the fight. Too, I heard the sad news of our Major's death at six o'clock this morning. There is not a man in the regiment but mourns his loss as a brave, humane and noble officer. The 19th is doomed to be the martyr of the second brigade. Captain Baker now commands the regiment, and we have but nine officers in the regiment. Lieutenant Coblentz is sick again, which leaves me sole commander of Company E. It is a task I do not like to perform, but with good health I shall perform the duty with cheerfulness. Owing to the casualties of the few men I had with regiment, today the Captain sent me to join the company now on duty with the train. I found it a long and searching tramp to find the boys but succeeded at last and now enjoy the quiet and peace of a rear guard, and how strange it seems to be where I cannot hear the musketry fire; but still we are not far enough in the rear to be out of hearing of the cannon and the bursting of shell, telling too well that the strife is still going on, and that all of Uncle Sam's boys are not enjoying the peace and quiet that I do. I would to God they did. Our lines are steadily advancing. We take one Rebel breastwork by storm, then another and another, and so on, and I expect this kind of fighting will last until we reach the river, which is in between the Rebel rear and Atlanta. The first time I have been lonesome in a long time was today, when I found I had lost three men out of nine that I had with me. My heart was made glad when I was ordered to join the company, and to-night I am at home. It seemed so good to get with the boys once more.

June 17

Last night was the first night I have not been awakened by the roar of battle in the month. We heard some artillery, but it was a long way off. The forenoon we passed at leisure, and the company enjoyed the rest, but I, being in command of the company, had plenty to do that kept me busy. At noon the train was ordered up closer to the ranks of our victorious army. It was a long time getting under way, but at last we were under motion. Its length was so great that we were seven hours in moving two miles. The train went into park between the lines of the breastworks, so we are now upon the ground that was a battlefield a few hours ago. The Rebel works and ours are hardly ten rods apart at this place. There is not a tree nor a bush but has the mark of a bullet upon it. The trees have many. At about four o'clock the artillery fire opened all along the line. Volley after volley was fired, and shell after shell burst in the distance, keeping up a constant roar. I thought I had heard loud artillery firing, but never so terrific before. Nor did night close the strife. The sky was overcast at nightfall.

The rain descended in torrents. The right wing of the army has advanced some distance today, but not being at the front I do not know their exact position. The losses have been considerable today, for the long ambulance trains have passed us all day laden with the wounded. I am somewhat hardened to the soldier's life, but I was surprised to see how patiently the wounded boys bore their pains.

June 18

All night I was kept awake by the roar of artillery and musketry. It being moonlight, the battle did not cease, though it rained all night. Today the battle has been more fierce than any I have listened to in this campaign. What the results have been is more than I know, but the lines do not appear to have advanced a great way. It has been a steady and constant roar all day. I have been drawing rations and attending to the company until I am wet to the skin. In short, it has been anything but pleasant either in mind or body. I find it more disagreeable to be where I can see the marks of battle and see the suffering than it is to be upon the front line. The works that we have just gained or taken from the Rebs are far superior to our own and far better than any I have seen. They were built by citizens and negroes and are of green logs and banks of earth to the thickness of six or eight feet and barbetted too. Their works were enfiladed so that they were as strong as man could make them. I wonder how they were ever driven out of them. Our lines were advanced so close to theirs that it would seem almost impossible for our boys to build their own works, but the impudent Yankees will venture almost

anything, and with their training in the art of war they
will accomplish almost any task they undertake to perform. I notice that all along the Rebel works the ball
marks are plentiful, showing that our men fired accurately and must have done a great deal of execution. I
noticed particularly the position of a Rebel battery,
where our battery had thrown shell at them. Not a ball
of ours struck their works, but came so close to the bar-
bette that they cut out the stakes and gun carriages of
the Rebel guns and must have done great execution.

June 19

It rained all night, and today it has been cloudy and
gloomy. The mud is deep and plentiful. At noon the
train was ordered up. Our corps having advanced some
two miles with difficulty, the long and heavily laden
train moved about one and one-half miles. The stalling
and tipping over of wagons was frequent, and the boys
worked hard to right them up. We were all the afternoon going the above distance and should have gone
farther, but, coming to a little stream swollen by the recent rains, we had to stop and bridge it, which took until
a late hour. We encamped upon a nice sod and have a
good prospect of sleep and rest tonight. The battle has
been progressing. As for the few days past, we have
gained ground slowly, and tonight we are at the base of
Twin Mountains. They are a beautiful scene. I cannot
help but admire their grandeur, though it is amid a
scene of death and destruction. They rise many feet
above the level and stand alone. Their name, I suppose,
originated because they are so near of a size and so close
together. It was but a few hours ago that the Rebel

headquarters were upon their summits. Being away from the regiment, I do not know what they are doing, though I doubt not but they are doing their part.

June 20

All day it has rained, and all day we have lain in camp within close hearing of the battle that is in progress. Some charging has been done and some severe firing. They do not appear to have advanced the lines very far, or none at all. The Johnnies fight hard here. It appears our forces are on three sides of them, and in the rear of them is the river, which is much swollen by the recent rains; so they are somewhat obliged to fight. The time passes slowly and drearily, but we shall be relieved tomorrow and again join the regiment where the battle is raging. I hope it may be better weather, and I hope for success. There is a kind of dread about this train that I do not like nor cannot account for. I believe I shall be better satisfied with the regiment. I received a letter from home today that did me good.

June 21

It is raining again today with little prospect of its stopping. About noon the train was ordered forward, as the corps had moved to the right. We were all the afternoon and until nine o'clock P.M. going three miles. The mud was axeltree-deep most of the way and the road full of dead horses and mules; but we have a good place to camp tonight and a good bed of pine boughs to sleep upon. We were not relieved as we expected, and now it is uncertain when we will be. The lines have advanced today, taking two lines of Rebel works that were stronger if anything than those that were taken on Sunday. With their entrenchments and embankments, it seems impossible to charge and take such works, yet sometimes our boys do it, but the greater part of them are taken by General Sherman's flank movements. Thus the battle is prosecuted, and we are gaining ground slowly day by day.

June 22

This morning dawned clear and bright. The sun shed its clear and brilliant light over the eastern hills for the first time in many days. It is too lovely a day to be engaged in the work we are in, but at an early hour there was a general advance all along the line. The 2nd division was the first to be engaged and, of course, our brigade. The roar of musketry was terrific along the entire line. About noon the wounded began to arrive at the hospital, which is situated close to our camp. There were a good many from the 19th Michigan, among the number Lieutenant Shafer of Company A wounded in the thigh; showing only too painfully that the tattered and torn regiment has again done its part towards punishing the enemy. The roar and tumult of battle ceased only as darkness compelled it. Our forces gained a position they have been aiming at for the last four days and now can shell Marietta with ease. There is an amusing incident that the 4th Army Corps performed today that is upon every tongue and worthy of note. When they were ordered to charge, each man leaped their works, and, taking a rail from the fence in front of their works, proceeded upon the double quick to the Rebel works. The Rebs fled from their works with wonder and dismay, but the boys, not content with taking one line of works, pushed on to the second line, where the Rebs made a stand. The boys formed breastworks of their rails under their very noses, despite their heavy fire, and in a few moments made their fire too hot for the Johnnies, and they fled in disorder from their second line of works. The 20th Corps did its share of charging too, exposing at one time our brigade to capture, but by the foresight of Colonel Coborn was brought off in time to save them. This information I have from the wounded. I have not been in engagement as we are not relieved yet. We are with the train, where the sound of battle is more terrible, if anything, than it is where the balls are flying. Although the boys are busy the most of the time with the train, they are uneasy and act as though they are out of their place. Many of them express the wish to return to the regiment, but for my part I am content to remain for some days. In front of the 20th Army Corps occasionally the pickets exchange a shot. At one point we passed the Twin Mountains directly under the Rebel guns. They had shelled our train the day before from their works, but our boys got range upon their guns with some parrotts, which soon silenced the Rebel guns, and they were kept so by our boys firing a shell every five minutes into the Rebel works. Last night the Rebels made another desperate charge to break our lines, but as before were unsuccessful. Our boys piled them up in heaps in front of their works. I found E. I. Mugg at the shanty and learned of William's death and other information of the boys that were left back. I had a good visit with him. He gave me a sanitary shirt (cotton) and some writing paper, too. I had a good dinner of peach pie, gingerbread and coffee.

June 23

The day has been bright and clear, but oh! how warm and sultry. The boys have passed the time leisurely reclining beneath the cool shade of some high pine tree or by the cooling stream, bathing frequently. As for myself, I have passed the time in writing. There appears to be a lull in the battle today, except for an occasional booming of a cannon to remind us that the two armies still oppose each other; but at six o'clock P.M. the Rebels made an assault upon our lines upon the right where we were not in position, but so nearly so that we gained our position first, and in the short space of twenty minutes breastworks were built and a battle fought. Old Joe's boys and a part of the 4th and 23rd Corps repulsed the Johnnies, killing and wounding over two thousand of them. Our loss was small. The Rebs were trying to flank us upon the right but failed in every effort. Old Joe and Schofield were too wide awake for them.

June 24

This morning the train moved to the right in the same direction as the corps moved yesterday. Though the train moved early in the morning, it was warm and sultry. The train parked in an open field about nine o'clock, and the remainder of the day was passed in fixing up our quarters and lying about in the shade. I busied myself with company affairs and had but a little rest. There

was a lull in the battle storm today along the entire line
until late in the evening, when there was a heavy cannonading. The works have been strengthened and new
dispositions of troops have been the order of the day.
We received mail tonight, and I have later dates from
home. We are too busy here to think of anything but the
war that is before is and the presidency this fall. The
soldier is invariably for Abe and Andy. We still remain
with the train, and we are enjoying ourselves.

June 25

Again today the sun shines intensely hot, but we have
a little something to do that makes the lonely time pass
more swiftly. While the boys have been scouring their
guns, I have been busy with company returns, monthly
reports and descriptive lists. In short, I have sat in the
shade and sweat from the mere exercise of writing.
While it was cool this morning, I went to a swamp and
gathered huckleberries enough for a mess and some
grapes, and today I have lived upon coffee, hard bread
and sauce. There has been some skirmishing along the
line today and heavy cannonading upon the extreme
left. There is considerable activity along the lines preparing for the harder fighting that must come soon; but I
have been confined to my pen all day and must now go
to the quartermaster and get some blanks and papers
for the morrow and to get the news, if any. I have seen
and heard less of war today than in the last two months.

June 26

The day has been as warm and uncomfortable as yesterday and a little more disagreeable from the fact that we were obliged to go out in the sunshine and have inspection of arms. I have busied myself with returns and receipt rolls of the company and have been busy all day. At evening we had a sermon in camp, and the minister preached the principle of hell fire and damnation in true Methodist style. It did very well for a change in our monotonous mode of life. The skirmishing still goes on in front, but neither army advances. There seems to be a lull in the strife, or rather a waiting for some other action. It is reported and generally believed that Rosecrans is coming up from the Mississippi upon our right with forty thousand men. If he does, (and he was known to be at Rome, Georgia, three days ago (we will give the Johnnies thunder in this quarter. I had huckleberries and blackberries for dessert today.

June 27

This day has been another very warm and sultry one. I have passed the day in writing and preparing the company for the coming muster. I find in making my rolls that the missing are many, and the writing of their names and the remarks opposite each absentee's name reminds me of the losses of the company. Eighty-two names I have written upon the roll and but twenty-six men answer to those names. Sometimes I am discouraged, but I am so busy that I soon forget the thought and attend to those that are present for duty. The cannonading has been kept up all day at short range, and there has been a considerable skirmishing but appearantly too little or no effect. Towards evening Lieutenant Barnhart, Company C, and I went to the regiment on business and to see the boys. We had a good visit, but several times we were greeted by a whistling ball or the bursting of a shell. The boys were in the second line, but close enough to the Johnnies for me.

June 28

The days begin to be monotonous. We occupy the same lines we did a week ago and sleep upon the same spot of ground, but for all it is monotonous and warm, I am busy enough with muster rolls and company affairs. I have shoved my pen all day upon a cracker box, and I am as tired as thunder. I should not mind the labor, if I had a decent place to write, but this, I suppose, is one of the pleasures of soldiering. I was at the regiment today. The pickets keep up the same ceaseless round of firing, and the whistling of balls sounded natural enough as I passed along the line. The boys are lying in the second line of works and have become somewhat used to lying upon the ground, ever ready with gun in hand to fight the Rebels.

June 29

Today, the same as yesterday, we are upon the same ground and performing the same kind of duty. I have been writing all day and until eleven o'clock P.M. By persevering I finished my company papers and have got the boys ready for muster, and though they have ragged clothes, they are clean and their guns are in good order. If they do not pass inspection and muster, it will not be my fault. At evening I drew a blouse, and the Captain

gave me a cap, so I can dress up. Yet my pants are ragged, but I shall have time to patch them now, as I have
my company affairs all straightened up. The regiment
occupies the same line and are under the same fire as
yesterday. The boys lie about as unconcerned as though
they were playing a game of ball upon a schoolhouse
green. General Butterfield was relieved from the command of our division and ordered to Washington today.
What it was for I do not know, but suppose it was for
incompetency.

June 30

Today is general muster, and a warm day it is. The
boys came out in full uniform, and oh! how they sweat.
There is a general murmuring among them. I took my
rolls and returns up to the regiment early this morning
and mustered Company E by proxy, so the boys were
not called out into line. Upon my return to the company, I was detailed to go with a squad to the big shanty

"I was detailed to go to Big Shanty for rations.

for rations. It was about two o'clock when we started,
and it was raining a brisk shower. Mounting a government wagon, we rode to the left and close to our lines

until we reached the station, as it is called, and there was
a lone cotton shed to mark the spot. Though it was alive
with Yankees who were handling army supplies, all
along the lines there was the same quiet that has pre-
vailed.

July 1

How strange it seems to greet the month of July here
in the wilderness of Georgia, but here we are fighting
our way through the woods and over the mountains. I
have been busy all morning running about the station
and have found two others of the company boys and
had a good visit, though I am tired, and it is very warm.
At noon the train was loaded, and we started back. The
sun was intensely hot, and as we were obliged to march,
it made hard work for us. I think I never sweated so before, and I never want to sweat so again. My shoes are
full of water, and my feet blistered. I was a glad boy
when I got into camp, but my work was not done. As
soon as I had got off my wet clothes (the boys were
drawing clothes, so I drew a full suit) and washed up I
had to take my pen and write in the company books
until dark. Sleep will be sweet tonight, for I am tired,
and it is cool, so we can rest well.

July 2

Today I have been sewing most of the time. There
was a portion of the day that I issued clothing to the
boys, but it was a short job. In the afternoon I gathered
some blackberries and had some sauce for supper. The

forenoon was very warm, but in the afternoon there were frequent showers, so we enjoyed ourselves. There is a great deal of moving of troops to the right today, but we remain in our old position. The 14th and 15th Army Corps are moving to the right, but what the object is I do not know. I only know they are obeying General Sherman's orders, and, if they are properly executed, they cannot fail to accomplish something. I have some hope this fight will soon be ended. Artillery firing has been kept up all day and all along the lines. The boys are dressed in new clothes today and look like themselves once more.

EDITOR'S NOTE: *Sherman had become convinced that it was impossible to bring all his armies to bear at once in the rugged Georgia terrain. He therefore kept pressure on the Rebs and continued his advance by an unending series of flanking movements. He hoped that the Confederates, eventually, could no longer afford to retreat and would be forced to stand or utilize aggressive tactics.*

The Union armies were now less than 10 miles from Atlanta.

July 3

Between the hours of eleven and twelve o'clock last night, the battle opened in all its fury upon the left of the line. It was nothing but a skirmish at first, but soon volley after volley of musketry was heard upon the night air, and ere many minutes the artillery was opened, and the unearthly sound mingled with the roar of small arms and the victorious shout ringing above all made a dismal sound upon the stillness of the night. It was of short duration, however, running down the line to the right for nearly two hours. Suddenly the fire slackened, then I distinctly heard the order to cease firing, and the next moment there arose three deafening cheers, telling me plainly that our boys had again driven the Rebs. As the gray light of morning lit the eastern sky, the army was in pursuit of the retreating Rebels, and tonight we are encamped beyond Marietta. Scarcely had the troops started before the train was in motion, and passing through a belt of woodland (as usual) a distance of ten miles, the train parked in an open field for the night. I can hear the artillery tonight, but it is a long way in front of us. We should have moved some farther tonight, but finding the hills so steep it retarded our progress so much that we were unable to reach our destination. In passing the Rebel works, I noticed the ball marks of our batteries. They were low and evidently did great execution. Their works were literally torn to pieces by our shot and shell. The day has been unusually warm and sultry. Several of the boys were sun struck, besides some being wounded. The weather is so warm that we are obliged to move slowly and rest often.

July 4

The first sound that greeted my ears this morning was the salute of cannon all along the lines, but not exactly a national salute, because they were sending their deadly missiles after the retreating Rebels. At the gray of dawn we again advanced but soon found the Rebels in position and waiting for us. Our lines came up in good order under General Sherman in person, but no fighting was done save upon the skirmish line and the artillery. Troops have been moving to the right all day, so there is something going on that I do not know of. The 19th, 20th and 23rd Army Corps, with a corps of cavalry, moved to the right at a late hour, and by morning may be in Atlanta, but as no one knows where they were going or where they will stop, we must await patiently the results of the expedition. It is the ever eventful day of the 4th of July, and what a world of events have transpired since the familiar old day greeted us one year ago. As for the day, I was up early, and the train moved about a mile, then went into park. The guard camped in the edge of the woods, where I have made myself comfortable. I went out berrying and found grapes and blackberries in abundance. The evening I passed in making some company receipt rolls for clothing. Although the merry dance and delicacies of home have not been mine to enjoy, I have been contented and happy.

July 5

Today the army advanced again through a dense wilderness as is usual but found the Rebels very strongly entrenched, too strongly to attack in front. It seems General Sherman has again flanked them out of another of their strongholds. Their works were of the strongest kind but have not been built so long as those at Lost Mountain and Twin Mountains. After the Rebels had been driven out of their works, they retreated towards the river several miles with our army close upon their heels. Company E with the train had all it could do to keep up. It has been so warm a good many of the boys have fallen in the ranks from heat. Lieutenant Lilly had a sun stroke and probably will not recover. We are close to the Chattahoocha River, and they are fighting upon its banks. I shall hear the firing of the cannon the last thing tonight.

July 6

It was early this morning when the train was under motion. After moving about four miles we found we were upon the wrong road, but fortunately the 20th Army Corps moved to the left of the lines, passing close to the park. At night we moved still farther to the left in the rear of our division and parked about ten o'clock. There is some skirmishing along the line, but nothing more. The Rebels are now upon their last foothold this side of the Chattahoocha, and ere many days we shall be going for Atlanta, which is in plain sight from our lines, though it is some distance off. I can see the place only by the aid of a field-glass. The Rebels are now in their last line of works, and we may have some hard fighting before we drive them much farther, but General Sherman is enough for the Johnnies yet.

July 9

This morning I again visited the regiment, where I received four letters, which made me company for the remainder of the day. Though I have been busy all day with the company books, I have found time to read them and answer three of them. There was some firing in the front today, caused by the 23rd Army Corps crossing the Chattahoocha. They succeeded, however, with-

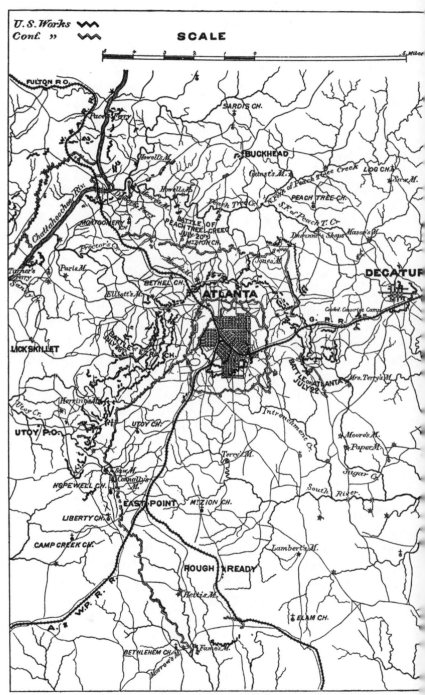

The approaches to Atlanta

out the loss of a man, so the Johnnies will have to dig out again or be fired upon in the rear, too. I visited a hill, where with the aid of a field-glass I could see the doomed city of Atlanta. General Sherman will take the place by slow siege this warm weather. Its capture is but a question of time now.

July 10

Today has been usually quiet and warm. Indeed, it seems monotonous enough, though I have been busy all day. I have been writing most of the time. Early in the morning I was out gathering berries and have had some rare dishes of fruit for dinner and supper. It has been unusually quiet all along the lines today, and the boys are bold enough to go to and from the picket line for berries. Both parties seem to have mutually agreed not to fire upon each other, and while the Rebs are upon the south bank and our boys upon the north bank of the river, they have changed papers, traded coffee for tobacco etc. Lieutenant Coblentz returned tonight but is unfit for duty.

July 11

Early this morning I was off for berries, and at sunrise a terrific musketry broke out upon the right of the line and extended to the left, which hurried me back to camp; but the fight was a short one, and by nine o'clock all was quiet, and the boys were swimming with the Rebs as they were yesterday. By agreement, they threw down there arms and agreed upon an armistice for the remainder of the day. Where I am with the train a stranger would think there was not a Rebel within a hundred miles of camp, but they are as thick as grasshoppers in a hay field. I have busied myself by writing and making out the payrolls. It has been warm as usual, but threatening rain.

July 12

Today has been monotonous, the weather warm and showery. I have been busy with making out the payrolls all day. Sergeant Lock joined the company again today and is as lively as ever. His wounds are healed, and he is all right. There has been but little doing at the front. The pickets have agreed upon another armistice, and the pickets from both armies are having as good a time as a lot of schoolboys just let loose from school. I presume tonight they will be shooting at each other. There are but few rumors afloat today and no news. There is nothing going on that I can hear of. In short the storm of battle has assumed a quiet that seems impossible, but strange things happen in this war.

July 13

It is quiet again today. The Rebs have moved their pickets back from the river bank. It is supposed they were getting too intimate with our boys. And, indeed, they were becoming friendly, proving to me clearly that if the privates of both armies were turned loose they would settle this war in a hurry. There was some artillery firing upon the right. Towards night two corps crossed the river upon the left and occupied a hill where they are now fortifying. I have busied myself with making out the payrolls. The day was warm as usual. Wesley Lock returned today and was promoted to first Sergeant, C. B. Rodebaugh promoted to Sergeant, and T. G. Rice, C. I. Compton and Henry Holdeman promoted to Corporals.

EDITOR'S NOTE: *On July 17th, General Johnston, the Rebel commander, received a telegram from Confederate President Davis as follows:*

I wish to hear from you as to present situation, and your plan of operation so specifically as will enable me to anticipate events.

Johnston answered on the same day but his answer was considered unsatisfactory and evasive by President Davis. The following day, Confederate Adjutant General Cooper telegraphed Johnston:

I am directed by the Secretary of War—as you have failed to arrest the advance of the enemy to—Atlanta, and express no confidence that you can defeat or repel him, you are hereby relieved from the command of the Army and the Department of Tennessee, which you will immediately turn over to General Hood.

July 17

It has rained all night, and the morning is bright but cool and lovely, inviting the boys to roam for berries, etc. Inspection is announced for nine o'clock A.M., and the boys are busy cleaning their guns and accoutrements. Many a merry joke was cracked, and, as I feel like myself this morning, I have taken a part with the boys in their merriment. At eight o'clock A.M. it was announced that we were relieved as train guards and ordered to join the regiment. A few moments sufficed to put us on the road. On arriving at the regiment we found their camp evacuated and learned that they were on picket. The 20th Army Corps is under marching orders for three o'clock this P.M., and we are waiting for the time to roll around. The 23rd Regiment Massachusetts Volunteers relieved us at the train. Moving to the left, we crossed the railroad and went thence to the river, passing down the former lines of our troops, but they have nearly all crossed the river before us, so the grounds were vacant. Crossing the river upon the pontoons, we passed the 14th Army Corps and the 1st Division of our corps, and at eleven o'clock P.M. we bivouacked for the night by the roadside. We have marched in all nearly twelve miles and now are nearing the extreme left of the line. I am so nearly given out that I must rest.

July 18

Waiting until about twelve o'clock noon in breathless suspense, our columns were in motion. Crossing a creek we formed in mass by brigade. Then we advanced through the woods to the Marietta and Atlanta road but found no Rebs. Then, moving down the road by column in platoon, we marched some ways and found the 4th Army Corps in front of us. After marching about six miles we filed to the right into a heavy woodland and bivouacked in line of battle for the night. We have made a great advance today, farther than I expected to without a fight. Now we are within six miles of Atlanta, but there is room between here and that place for a big fight yet. Generals Sherman, Thomas, and Hooker are with us constantly, and all are confident of final success. The day has been clouded and cool, otherwise we would have suffered greatly from the heat. As it was, we sweat freely, but the boys stood the trip nobly. I feel better tonight, but am still tired and weary and need rest greatly. The country has been hilly and poorly cultivated.

July 19

This morning finds us lying behind our guns in the same line we had formed last night. Before sunrise the bugle sounded reveille. In a few moments the whole line was ablaze with camp fires upon which the boys were cooking breakfast. Early in the morning we had orders to be ready to march at a moment's notice, and patiently we have waited all day, but tonight finds us in the same line with our guns in the same stacks. The several bands are making music gaily, as if they were in Michigan, and, indeed, there is but little danger where we now are; for from observation I find there are other lines in front of us, which have been skirmishing with the Rebs all day, but with what results I do not know. This much I do know; Atlanta is closely invested and soon must fall, or we must fight.

EDITOR'S NOTE: *On the evening of July 19, the Union right was attacked by Hood while they were crossing Peachtree Creek on the outskirts of Atlanta. The attack was repulsed. This was the Battle of Peachtree Creek.*

Peach Tree Creek from General Hooker's position

July 20

This is another eventful day long to be remembered by the heroes of the day. At early dawn we moved to the front. Many a boy melted beneath the scorching rays of the southern sun, but about noon we formed upon the left of the 2nd Division and joined the 4th Corps on the right. We were closed in column by division in an open field and lay down behind temporary shade, but we had but little time to rest. At three o'clock it was announced along the line that the Rebs were charging upon us. They came down upon us in seven lines of battle, threatening the 3rd Division with destruction. No commanding officers seemed to be present. Our gallant Colonel Coburn ordered his brigade forward, swinging in to the left, which saved the whole division from retreat. By this time the roar of battle was loud and constant. In our turn we charged the Rebels, driving them back in confusion. Coming up to our former skirmish line, we halted and the battle was kept up until night, when the work of fortifying commenced. We worked all night, and a tireder and lamer set of men I never saw. I never suffered so from heat before. My clothes were as wet as though I had been in water. Our loss was comparatively light. Three men from my company were wounded, which is about the average, but the Rebels suffered dreadfully. In front of our regiment the boys have buried nearly two hundred, and thousands have been wounded. I noticed several places where the blood has run in steams down the hillside, and go where you will, there are pools of blood. It is a sickening and horrid sight such as I never wish to see again, though tomorrow may renew the strife. I find the engagement has been general all along the lines, and we are pressing Atlanta closely. McPherson and Schofield have swung in upon the left and are reported to be within a mile and a half of Atlanta.

July 21

After dark last night the 19th was relieved from the front line and went to the rear, where we built a temporary work and rested for the day, but I had been too fatigued and too tired to rest in one day, so tonight I feel quite poorly, in fact, I am sick; but there is some prospect of a good night's rest, so I may be better in the morning. The morning was passed by our troop in carrying off the dead and wounded. The 19th losses are

Action of July 22nd, 1864, the battle for Atlanta

five killed and thirty-five wounded, which is about an average of the whole loss, but the Rebs' loss is at least ten times ours. Five hundred were buried in front of our brigade, and our hospital is crowded with their wounded. We have a real bunch of prisoners. The day is very warm and sultry. It seems almost impossible for the men to endure such heat.

July 22

Early this morning the skirmish line advanced to the Rebel works and found them evacuated. The bugles all along our line sounded an advance. A few minutes sufficed to put the army in motion, and passing over the Rebel works, we advanced about a mile and a half and again came to another line of Rebel works. We did not advance closely enough to engage them with the musket, except the skirmishers. Halting, we began the work of fortifying and worked the remainder of the day. Tonight we can boast of the best line of earth works we ever built, but since we got into position the Rebs have shelled us vigorously, but did little damage. They silenced one of our batteries on an open hill, but by the morrow we will have such forts that it will bother the Rebs to silence our guns. The day has been warm, and many a boy has fallen from the effect of the scorching rays of the sun. I feel somewhat better, but still am very tired and fatigued. Wesley and Chris were overheated today and have gone to the hospital.

July 23

We have loitered about the works all day and enjoyed

ourselves hugely in eating, drinking and resting. But little has been done on the line today, save the building of forts and mounting of heavy guns. The skirmish line has kept up a continuous fire with little effect. There has been no mail received or sent out today, so the day has been a dull one. About sundown I was detailed for the skirmish line for the first time since I enlisted. Consequently I have a new lesson to learn. I only dread it because my eyes are so poor. But as I have been put on reserve I am all right for the night. The day has been clouded and cooler than usual, and the evening is very cool, but there is no rest for the pickets, so I have made up my mind to a night of wakefulness. I have written the above between two fires of musketry.

July 24

To me this has been the longest day of the season, it being my duty to keep awake during the night. It was tedious, and the roar of artillery and musketry caused the time to be more dreary and lonesome than it would otherwise have been. Some of the boys consider this rare sport and are laughing and shouting as well as shooting at the Rebs. The boys have some good pits and have a little the advantage in the ground, so our boys are pretty safe. None has been hurt as yet. At sundown the relief came in sight, and my heart was glad with the prospect of returning to camp, for I am tired and sick, and unless I get better soon, I must give up to disease. The night was very cold, and there was a heavy dew, almost a frost, and the day has been correspondingly warm, but Delos has supper ready for me, so I will eat and then lie down to rest.

July 25

This morning finds me still unwell and tired, so the day has been passed lying upon my blanket. I have written one letter only. The line of battle was advanced a few rods today, and the boys have busied themselves in digging their new entrenchments, and tonight finds us wallowing in the dirt, or, rather, sleeping in a ditch with the roar of artillery and musketry to lull us to sleep. The company is dwindling to nothing in number. Seventeen of our seventy-nine men are all we can muster for duty. The scurvy is making its appearance among the men, and many of them are coming down with it. There appears to be but little doing upon the lines, save the work of making them stronger. Artillery firing has been kept up at intervals, and there is constant firing upon the skirmish line. I hope I shall feel better tomorrow. At this time I must lie down.

July 26

I have felt a little better today and took a ramble to the rear to see the sick. I found Chris and Wes and pretty hard up they are, as well as other boys of the company. The day has been cloudy and cool for this climate, and I have enjoyed my tramp hugely though I have been unwell. Returning to the line, I found I was tired, and after eating a hearty supper of berries that I picked on the road, I lay down to rest, but did not rest a great while, for we received orders to strike tents and move to the right a mile and a half, which was promptly done, but it was hard work for me, and it was twelve o'clock at night before I again lay down. The 2nd Division of our corps relieved us from the line we occupied, and we are now in the rear, and I would to God we could stay here until the boys can recover.

July 27

It has been raining all day, and I am wet as well as unwell. Before noon we policed camp, and in the afternoon drew rations, the first I have drawn in some time, but Chris, Wes and Lew are sick, and the company has fallen back on Jack Lamb and myself as commanders. Our number is growing less and less every day, so much so that old Company E will not need a commander long. There is nothing doing in our front today, save the monotonous firing of the pickets. At one time the Rebs shelled us vigorously, but no one was hurt that I can hear of. It was quite a sight to see the duel. General Hooker was ordered to Washington this morning, and General Williams of Michigan now commands the 20th Corps. He has heretofore commanded the 1st Division of the corps. I dislike to part with Old Joe, but everything is for the best. General Williams is a good one, and we have no reason to complain. The 13th, 15th and 23rd Army Corps moved from the left to the right today, and some new scheme is on foot. Reinforcements have come up under command of General Rousseau. Time alone will develop our progress. The boys have been enjoying their rest greatly, and I notice it is a fine thing to be in reserve where one can sleep nights. Last night I slept the soundest that I have slept in two long weeks.

July 28

We are held in reserve yet, and it has been a lazy day, though an eventful one. The day dawned cloudy and gloomy, and the day passed slowly by until one o'clock P.M., when the three corps that moved to the right had got into position, and the Rebels attacked them in full force. Our boys sat about listening to the sullen roar until five o'clock P.M., when we received orders to march to the right and support General J.C. Davis' division of the 14th Corps, which was being hotly pressed. We marched at quick time and traveled about two miles of the distance, when we received the glad tidings that we were not needed and were ordered back to our old camp, where we have bivouacked for the night. We have no report of the battle yet today, other than that the Rebs were whipped at every point. I am still unwell and must rest.

The battle at Ezra Church

EDITOR'S NOTE: *On the 28th, General Howard was marching from the left wing to the right to extend the Union lines south and west of Atlanta when the Rebels attacked the Union flank at Ezra Church. They were again repulsed.*

In those battles, just before the capture of Atlanta, the Rebels lost 15,000 men while the Union armies lost about 6,000.

At this point General Sherman halted his plan to move his entire army upon Atlanta and flanked, then completely encircled the city during the next month.

July 29

Early this morning we were again ordered to march to the extreme left to support General J.C. Davis' division of the 14th Army Corps. We have marched a distance of eight or ten miles through the broiling sun, and many a boy has fallen out by the roadside unable to go any farther. I was obliged to fall out for the first time upon this campaign, and I suffered a great deal. If I were at home, I should lie down and call myself sick. The Lieutenant and Sergeant ———— were unwell and did not go with us, so the company command fell back upon me again. On our march today we passed the battlefield of yesterday of the 14th, 15th, and 16th Army Corps, and I find our victory was greater than I expected. The Rebs were slaughtered dreadfully, and many of them lie upon the ground unburied. Our loss was considerable but light when compared to that of the Rebels. I am tired out and sick tonight, but I am alone with the company and must attend to their wants.

July 30

I awoke this morning only to find that I am as unwell

and unfit for duty as I was last night. I find, too, that our whole division is upon the extreme right guarding the flank, which is no desireable job, and I heartily wish myself back with the 20th Corps where I belong. We lay about in the shade until noon, when the lines were advanced about eighty rods, and we were all the afternoon getting our position. It was a shame and wrong to keep us lying in the hot sun so long, and there was a general murmur among the men. I believe the commanding officers were all drunk. We were finally closed in mass by division in column and lay down for the night. There are rumors of another battle upon the left today, but nothing official. My eyes are very sore tonight, and I fear they will soon lay me up.

July 31

We have remained in camp all day, but have been under marching orders to support a reconnoitering party, but fortunately for us we were not needed. About noon it commenced raining, and, though it has cooled the air and made many a glad heart, it has been a gloomy day. Although it is Sunday, a day of rest, I have been very busy with monthly returns and reports and have them but partially completed. Wes and Chris came up to the company again today but poorly fitted for duty. There has been but little doing along the lines today. All is seemingly quiet, but the storm may break forth in its wild fury before another day passes. The struggle for Atlanta seems to progress slowly, but we have held every inch of ground we have gained, but the time passes tediously and slowly. My eyes are quite poorly today.

August 1

Welcome, new month, and haste the coming year, that the time may pass as swiftly as the past year has and bring the present crisis to a satisfactory end. There seems to have been but little done along the lines today. An occasional musket shot is all that has been heard, and the boys have felt a little secure and rested accordingly. A good many of them are sick, and the number is increasing daily. There is no news from any quarter today. I have passed the time in writing receipts and issues of ordinance and making monthly returns for Lieutenant Coblentz, who has resigned and is going home tomorrow. Towards night we moved camp a few rods to have a better ground. It is raining some tonight, cooling the air so we can sleep tonight with some comfort.

August 2

We have remained encamped today. The boys have cleaned their guns and clothes, as well as enjoyed pastimes. I have passed the day in writing letters and making out descriptive lists for the wounded boys who are in the hospitals. About four o'clock P.M. the 23rd Corps passed us and took position on our right, thus relieving us on the flank. The bugle immediately sounded the assembly, and in a few moments our division was moving to the left. Marching about five miles we halted in the rear of the 14th Corps, spread down our blankets and slept for the night. Lieutenant Coblentz started home this morning, and I sent several letters with him to mail and my little watch to Maria. The Lieutenant was a good fellow, but he was no officer and I am glad he is gone. I have done his duty for a long time, and he has received the pay.

August 3

This morning early our division relieved the 2nd Division of the 14th Corps, which joined our corps upon the right, so we are now upon the front line, where again we hear the monotonous crack of the skirmisher's rifle and sleep with one eye open, to be in readiness for a charge from the Johnnies at any moment. After dinner Chris and I started on a visit to the 9th Indiana V.V. in the 4th Army Corps and had gotten nearly to our journey's end when they had to kick up a fight with the Rebs, so we had to come back without seeing the boys. We came back by way of the hospital and saw some of the sick boys. When we returned to camp we were tired enough. We ate our supper and were preparing to lie down to rest, when orders came to advance our lines, so we shall have to dig with shovel and pick all night with tired limbs.

August 4

All night we worked with the shovel and pick, and this morning finds us safely entrenched in our new line of works. When we had them completed and our breakfast eaten, we were ordered to build another line upon our right to fill a vacancy between us and the 3rd brigade. The boys are tired and worn out, but they work with a will that I did not expect of them, and tonight I do not know where or when I have seen so tired a set of men as the 19th, and yet they are lively and full of glee. The day has been intensely hot, and the boys are as wet with sweat as though they had been in the creek. The fore-noon I passed in doing company writing. Wes, Chris and I went to the hospital, where we found some of the afflicted, and they appear to be doing well. In the after-noon I used the pick and shovel. My eyes are quite poorly tonight, and there is poor prospect of their being any better.

August 5

There has been a good deal of dispute between the commanding officers about the occupation of the new line, but we were finally permitted to occupy the part of the line that we built. The Engineer gave us (the 19th regiment) praise, as he has before, for building the heaviest and best works upon the line. The day has been passed in fixing up camp and finishing our works. The boys have built arbors over the ditch to protect them from the scorching rays of the sun, and we hope to re-main here long enough to enjoy some of the fruits of our labor. There has been no particular change in the lines today. The right appears to have been engaged from the roar of artillery in that direction. There has been some demonstration along our line, but it ended in a skirmish fight. I am somewhat unwell yet today, but have worked all the day and am tired.

August 6

This day I have had to myself and passed the time in

writing letters. I put in good time. Several times I was disturbed by the attack upon the pickets, but each time I was happily disappointed, for I did not see the Rebs. The attack each time ended with the pickets, and I resumed my pen. Everything was quiet along the lines today, except the artillery dueling, which is every day alike in severity and constancy. But few of our boys are hurt with shell, and if our shells do no more harm to the Rebs than theirs do to us, I would propose that they cease firing and thus stop the disagreeable sound. At night a train of cars ran up to our lines from Marietta and brought up the mail and some convalescent soldiers. When the whistle was blown the boys answered by a long, loud and wild cheer that made the old hills about Atlanta shake. To see and hear the cars once more reminds one of home.

August 8

I was detailed to go on the skirmish line last evening, but fortunately enough for me, I did not go, for it has rained all night, but it will be my turn in a day or two. I shall expect it tonight. It has been a lazy, idle day, as well as lonesome. I have passed the time in writing the company records and writing letters. There is no change in the lines today. The skirmish line keeps up a constant fire as usual, but few shots have been fired by the artillery today. The Orderly Sergeant of Company B was mortally wounded today by a stray ball while standing upon the company parade ground. In looking over this diary, I find I have left out our positions in the different lines, which is an important item. I have them in my memory, but that will not enlighten the reader. We are now upon the right of the 4th Corps and on the left of the 15th Corps. The 3rd Division is on the right, the 2nd Division on the left, and the 1st Division in the center of the corps.

August 9

Today our forces have opened a vigorous cannonading upon the city of Atlanta, but with what result is not known. The 15th Army Corps and the 3rd Brigade of our division have been advancing the lines again today. Thus another step has been taken, and another ditch has been dug to the discomfiture of Rebeldom. There has been a detail from the whole division to build the line of works, and there is some severe talking among the boys about the affair, as we (the 2nd Brigade) have always built our own works. It brings the duty pretty thick and fast on the boys, and I do not blame them much. The forenoon I passed in doing official writing for the company at the Quartermaster's, and the afternoon I called my own and occupied it in writing and reading, which, by the way, was but little comfort, for my eyes pain me severely tonight on account of it. I am thankful that I do not have to go on picket.

August 10

I have been at work with the boys detailed on the works and was relieved at noon, but I find a man can get tired in a half day with using the pick and shovel. The Rebs opened their artillery upon us about noon, but the works were so far advanced that they did us but little damage. At evening, however, they opened a piece farther to the left, which completely raked the line, killing two men and injuring several others. The day has been rainy and cool, so we have been favored in our works. There has been no change in the line save that the reinforcements, General Stedman commanding, moved to the right with the 9th Michigan Cavalry. Too, some heavy ordnance came in upon the train today and will probably be put in position tonight. Thus we shall hear some big shelling soon. The usual picket and artillery firing has been kept up at intervals all day. Thus another day has passed, and another night is before us.

August 11

This day, like those that have preceded it, has been noted for its noise, confusion, and hard labor. All day the boys have been shoveling, and the pickets have kept up their incessant fire. One man from Company I was killed while out with the working party and one of Company G wounded. There appears to be a general advancing of the lines and getting into position of heavy ordnance. A furious cannonading opened in the night, which naturally kept a fellow awake. It has rained and is quite comfortable for this climate. The sun is hidden most of the time behind clouds, which makes it rather gloomy. There are rumors about the camp that Mobile is ours, but I do not credit the report. A new recruit came to the company today, T. D. Dewaters.

August 12

I have been somewhat unwell today but have been

writing most of the time. Nothing of importance occurred through the day save the routine of tedious toil upon the works. Too, they have kept up the usual skirmish fight. It is now twelve o'clock midnight, and I must hie to rest, for I am tired and unwell, too much so to notice what has been doing on the lines today. I believe the boys did move into the new works at night, but I shall stay in my old quarters.

August 14

Yesterday I was too ill to know what was going on around me, and today I do not feel much better, and my eyes are pretty bad tonight. The day has been a very quiet one until about five o'clock P.M., at which time a heavy fire opened on the right. What it was or what the causes were is more than I can learn, but it was continued only for a half hour, so it could not have been very severe. I have laid on my bunk for the last two days, so I am but poorly posted upon affairs that surround me, and even at this writing I am unfit to be sitting here, so down I go again on my bunk.

August 15

The day has been passed rather idly by us except upon the skirmish line, which was advanced at an early hour. They had quite a severe fight over their newly gained position, but our boys have held their own, and now have good pits and a good line. It would puzzle a line of battle now to drive in our skirmishers. Nothing unusual transpired along the line today, save the usual firing of artillery. In consequence of the scurvy prevail-

ing in camp, they have ordered no salt meat issued to
the men, and there is a great deal of murmuring among
the men. I cannot blame them, for hard bread and coffee is rather dry living. I feel somewhat better tonight,
but have laid on my bunk most of the day. The day
closed with a shower, and, it being cool, the boys got together to drive dull care away by singing, and it was late
before they retired.

August 16

It has been very quiet on our front today. Even the
pickets have fired but few shots, and they were aimed
high and for the rear. The boys have rare sport at times
on the skirmish line in shelling Atlanta. The musket is
double charged and then elevated to an angle of thirty
degrees. They are discharged sometimes by detail, sometimes by file, and sometimes by volley, and I doubt not
but many of the minié balls so fired light in the city.
Our skirmish line is very close to that of the Rebs, but
they seldom fire at each other. I have passed the time in
doing company writing and at evening went to the hospital to see some of the boys from the company. Matt
Daniels was about the same. There is no mail for us
today, and there is a report in camp that the railroad is
cut in our rear. I am feeling considerably better today.

August 17

The rumor in camp yesterday is confirmed this morning, and we learn that the railroad is cut near Dalton,
but a day or two will repair the damage. Communica-

tions are ordered stopped for two days both going and coming. This morning I was awakened by the screaming shell from the Rebs, but the firing soon ceased, and the artillery was silent the remainder of the day; but their skirmishers were busy with their muskets, and the little balls have been flying pretty thick and fast. Byron Dunn of the 9th Indiana came to our camp about ten o'clock and remained to dinner, when Chris and I went back to the 9th. We have been disappointed in finding Carlton and Cleveland, the former having died of wounds, the latter being also wounded and gone to the rear. Charles Peasley is all right. I see a good many familiar faces in the 9th, but I am puzzled to call them by name. As we are somewhat tired, we have concluded to stay all night in the 9th.

August 18

This morning I awoke and found myself in the self-same spot that I had laid down in last night. Byron Dunn had got breakfast ready, and it was a gay one. In addition to army rations, we had green corn and apple sauce. I ate heartily, and many a time home and friends were spoken of. They are making all sorts of demonstrations here in the 4th Corps, as if massing our forces here for an assault, but it is a feint to draw the Rebels' attention from the right of our line, where, I understand, the 23rd Corps is making an attack upon the Rebel lines. The right now rests within a mile and a half of the Macon, Mobile and Atlanta Railroad, and as soon as our forces succeed in taking this road, that soon will all Rebel communications be cut off. This appears to be the cause of the incessant strife on the right. We returned to our old camp about noon, where I spent the remainder of the day in writing and in general inspection.

August 19

I learn this morning that our boys were successful on the right yesterday, capturing and holding the Macon & Mobile Railroad, but at a fearful loss of life. The particulars of the fight I have not learned. I could only hear the constant roar of artillery and musketry, which was long continued and severe. I have passed the time in writing letters and reading newspapers. At evening one of our boys, A.E. Hollister, was mortally wounded by a stray ball from Rebeldom through the right shoulder. He was a good boy and one of the best of soldiers, and he is missed by all who knew him. I have been detailed for picket duty for the next twenty-four hours, and I expect a tedious and lonesome time of it, but as good fortune will have it, I do not come on picket very often. As I conclude this writing, I hear the renewal of the battle upon the right.

August 20

Last night was the gloomiest of my experience in this campaign. After getting on post last night, it commenced raining and continued all night. The night air was made thrice hideous by the roar of battle upon the extreme right, the squeaking of a thousand crickets, and forest insects and the hoot of the owl. The place was unpleasant and uncomfortable from the close proximity of the Rebs, who had no better manners than to shoot at us every move we made. Our boys returned the fire, but we could see nothing, consequently did but little or no execution. Both their line pickets and ours are upon the same hill and scarcely eight rods apart, but the summit of the hill hinders us from seeing one another. The night and day have worn away tediously enough. The boys tried to talk to the Johnnies, but they were silent and sullen, each time giving a shot for a word. On being relieved tonight, I was blind, tired and sleepy and glad to get to camp. There has been no fighting on the right for the last twelve hours and no tidings from the battle last night.

August 21

We have no tidings from the right yet. I slept soundly last night, but tonight I am feeling very poorly, indeed so much so that I fear an attack of fever. The forenoon I passed in writing, and by evening I felt so poorly that I went to the Surgeon for advice. He gave me some medicine and gave me strict orders to be quiet. On returning to my quarters, I felt worse, and my disease assumed the form of pneumonia; so a sleepless night of labor and misery awaits me. The day has been quiet, scarcely a shot being fired from either side, save our artillery which keeps up an incessant fire upon the city.

August 22

My illness increased last night until I was miserable indeed, but the early application of medicine had checked its progress, so that I feel somewhat better, though I am sore and lame, particularly my right side and eyes. I have stuck to my bunk like a brother and hope I shall be beyond danger of another attack by tomorrow. The day has been very quiet. From the stillness around it would seem that there are no Rebs in our front. Nevertheless, they are in front of us in force, so this only appears to be a lull in the storm. There is no news or change of affairs here.

August 23

Today I find myself a good deal better but still unfit for duty, particularly my eyes. They are inflamed, and I fear they are going to bother me. Nevertheless, I have made out some receipt rolls of company clothing and garrison equipage, so the old company is all right once more. Lieutenant Barnhart receipted me, and I have given him the company rolls. The day, as yesterday, has been very quiet. In fact, I have not heard a bullet from the Rebs today, which is very uncommon for us. There is no news or change from any quarter, except that the railroad is repaired, and we have received mail and rations. I feel rather poorly yet tonight and must hie to rest.

August 24

My eyes are very much inflamed this morning, and I am elected for another trip to the hospital. So says the surgeon. The 20th Army Corps is under marching orders and are all wondering where they can be going, but all is conjecture. No one knows, and I am pretty sure that no one is going to tell us what our destiny is.

EDITOR'S NOTE: *On the 25th of August, 1864, Sherman resumed his advance on Atlanta and the Confederates, after one counterattack, evacuated the city on the 1st of September.*

In the four months of the Atlanta Campaign Union losses were reported as 32,000 while Confederate losses were 35,000. In the field, the Union armies numbered 100,000 while the Rebels placed 20,000 troops on the line.

Sgt. Ham Coe had seen his last combat of the war. The war continued, of course, until the final capitulation on May 26th, 1865, when Confederate General Kirby-Smith surrendered his forces in Mississippi.

Ham's observations of the day President Lincoln was assassinated are unforgettable. He was discharged one month later and made his way home with $195.70 in his pocket—his entire mustering out pay.

The rest of the diary is, if anything, more fascinating than the first.

August 25

We find ourselves in the same line this evening that we were in yesterday and under the same orders. The Hospital has been ordered back across the Chattahoochee, and I am sent there by the surgeon. My eyes are growing worse fast, and I am now satisfied that a regular course at the hospital is necessary before they will improve much.

August 26

This morning the hospital was moved across the river. I was obliged to walk six miles, and it was a sorry old

walk for me. My eyes pain me almost beyond endur-
ance. There are no tents up and no tent to put up,
therefore I lie under a tree tonight. The corps has fallen
back to the south bank of the river and there taken position to guard the line of communication, while General
Sherman and the rest of the army are making one of
their cursed flank movements to the right and in all
probability will be next heard from upon the Macon and
Atlanta Railroad.

August 27

My eyes are very bad this morning, and the surgeon
has simply ordered me to bathe them in cold water. I
am now almost too blind to write. There are no tents up
yet, and I am soaking wet this morning, and it is still
raining.

August 28

My eyes were so painful this morning that I was obliged to take morphine, and still the surgeon gives me
no medicine. Such treatment in my condition would
make a preacher swear, and I notice I have done some
of that today and have finally succeeded in getting a
hearing from the surgeon in charge and am pretty well
provided for tonight.

September 20

Today has been the first that I have been able to get

out in the light since I came to the hospital. I have been to the regiment. The walk made me tired and lame. I found them busy with payrolls and expecting pay this week. In the interval that appears in my diary great events have transpired. Atlanta has fallen, and a battle has been fought at Jonesborough. The former was the result of a flank movement to the right on the second inst., while the battle was fought for possession of the Macon and Atlanta Railroad. It resulted in a complete victory to our arms. The Rebs were charged out of their works by the 14th Corps. This was on the third and fourth inst.

September 21

I did not accomplish my designs at the regiment yesterday and shall go again soon, probably tomorrow. I am somewhat lame, but the eyes are none the worse for my tramp yesterday. I am tired of this groaning place and wish for the time to come when I can go to the regiment to stay. I found the boys all right. They come on duty every other day, but the duty is light (Provost Guards), and they are much better off than they would be on the front line. I find, too, that they as a regiment are very highly complimented in the city for discipline and military appearance. The same was reported to General Slocum, commanding the 20th Corps.

September 23

Early this morning I went to the regiment in company with Charles Richardson of Battery M, 1st New York,

and had a good walk. I stopped at a barber shop and
was shaved by a live barber for the first time in five long
months. I found the boys as usual enjoying themselves. I
had a talk with Captain Easton and a good visit. I returned to camp again in the afternoon rather tired, but
feeling the better for my walk. My eyes are improving
very slowly in this damp weather. It has rained constantly this afternoon.

September 25

Another Sunday I have been the occupant of the hospital. The day has passed slowly and tediously as usual.
There has been some excitement in camp over the victories of General Sheridan in the Shenandoah Valley.
The day has been a plesant one and cool.

September 26

Another day has passed, and I find myself singing the
same song. Peace and quiet reign throughout the camps.
The 2nd Brigade was on review in the city, and I was
out to see them. It is a splendid sight to see a corps pass
a given point in review.

October 4

The Rebs are crossing the Chattahoochee River in our
rear today near Sandtown. They are in large force and
are bound to give us trouble. Rumors are many and wild
with reference to the same. Our forces are taking things

coolly and are rather expecting an attack on our front. The Rebs are reported tonight to be in the vicinity of Big Shanty and Kenesaw Mountain, but trains came through from Chattanooga today. There have been some forts and rifle pits laid out in and through the city, and the army is again engaged in active operations. My eyes are somewhat worse today. I fear they are not going to improve much this winter.

October 5

The army, save the 20th Army Corps, was in motion early this morning after the Rebs in our rear. General Sherman left this morning, and General Thomas went north some days ago and is now coming this way with a heavy force. The Johnnies have, I fear, got the worse of the bargain this time. General Sherman will whip them worse than ever before. There is no news today but great activity in building the works through the city. I was at the regiment and drew some clothing. The boys were ordered to hold themselves in readiness for action at a moment's notice.

October 6

It is raining very hard today, nevertheless the work goes on. We received from General Sherman the news that he had captured two hundred wagons of the Rebel train and some six hundred prisoners, whom he has put to work repairing the railroad that they had just torn up. We are still expecting an attack upon the city, but the boys are as unconcerned as though they were at

Union bivouac in Atlanta

home. There is no news tonight, in fact, everything has come to a dead calm. As a calm always precedes a storm, so I look upon the surroundings of the city tonight, and there is no telling what quarter the storm may break from first or whether it will be a shower of bullets or a flood of good news.

October 8

Were I to record the events of today they would be the same as those of yesterday. Indeed, we are two hundred miles into the heart of Rebeldom with the enemy on all sides of us. Our "Cracker line" is interrupted or the railroad torn up, so we have had no mail for a long, long time. In truth, the army, save the 20th Army Corps, is fighting its way back over the same ground that it has just passed over, and all we have to do is to wait patiently for General Sherman to clear the road, though it is hard times with us to get no mail nor news. The work of fortifying the city is going on rapidly and approaching completion.

October 9

Today it is cold and blustery, but the day has been a cheering one for us. We received the news of General Sherman's victory at Altona Mountain, Rebel loss two thousand, our loss six hundred. The Rebs were completely routed and are retreating towards Lost Mountain, Alabama. Thus the railroad is once more cleared of Rebs, and we can look for better times soon. Too, our victory at Altona saved four thousand cattle that were on the road for this place (Atlanta) to supply the army with beef. It is cold enough for frost tonight, but the day has been clear and warm. To begin the week my eyes are no better than they were a week ago.

October 10

There was considerable excitement produced this morning by the Doctor's announcing in each ward that Richmond had fallen, but the excitement died away by noon, and I found that the atmosphere was just as cold and the hospital just as lonesome as in days gone by. However, the prospect of reopening the railroad in our rear is cheering, and God speed the day, for the boys at the regiment are living upon one and one-half pounds hard bread per day. It is tough for the boys, but they submit without a murmur. It would not be so bad if the fatigue duty upon the defenses of the city were not so heavy. There is no additional news tonight.

October 14

A glorious day this has been. Trains came through from Chattanooga and brought our mail. I have a pocket full of letters and have feasted on them all day, but the news tonight is discouraging again. Hood and his army are at Resaca in full force. Thus communications are again cut off.

October 17

Wild rumors are afloat again today of the Rebs having possession of the railroad at or near Resaca, and, as there have been no trains through for two days, I am inclined to believe the report. The foraging parties were attacked yesterday and had quite a skirmish and were reinforced today by two brigades.

October 18

Reports that were afloat yesterday were confirmed today, only they are not quite so bad as represented yesterday. From ten to fifteen miles of railroad are again torn up in our rear near Ringgold, Georgia. The day is as monotonous with me as usual. I write no letters because of the fact that they cannot be mailed, and I am not yet able to read, so the time passes slowly. The Indiana sick who have received furloughs and have

awaited transportation so long have received the same
and started today, so there is a prospect of the railroad
being open soon.

October 19

Today there is but little excitement or news. The 2nd
Brigade is coming in all right with six hundred wagons
loaded with forage with a loss of only two or three men.
There has been an order promulgated today sending all
convalescents north of the Tennessee River. My name
was taken as one of the number, and I hope I shall get
where I can get something to eat before long. The poor
beef and hard bread here is not the food for me to get
well on.

October 22

This morning we started on our trip northward and
got within five miles of Marietta, where a train had been
burned last week, and the engine, tender and one car
ran off the track. It has taken all the remainder of the
day to repair the damage, but if nothing happens we
will be rolling again by sundown.

October 23

We arrived at Resaca in the night somewhat tired.
This morning I started on foot for Dalton, a distance of
fifteen miles, to pass the break in the railroad, and it
was a big tramp for me. I observe here that Hood did a

good job tearing up the railroad. The destruction was complete, but our boys are fast repairing it. I arrived at Dalton at dark, made some coffee for those that were sick, and find myself tired and lame, but I have volunteered to stay up most of the night with the sick.

Hood (Confederate General) did a good job of tearing up the railroad.

October 24

This morning we are on the railroad again bound for Chattanooga, via Cleveland on the Knoxville road. We arrived at Chattanooga at four o'clock P.M. and were sent to General Field Hospital No. 2, where I now have a good bunk and good quarters. We had no trouble today upon the railroad, but loading the sick ones this morning and waiting on them through the day was a hard job, and I have not been so tired this summer as I am tonight. My eyes are somewhat worse for wear, but I hope they will be all right ere long.

October 28

This forenoon I went downtown and saw Major Baker, and at one o'clock I started for Nashville. Thus I shall be riding all night.

October 29

I arrived at Nashville this morning and repaired to Hospital No. 8, Ward 4, where I shall rest awhile, I hope. There are a good many receiving furloughs here, and I must try my hand at it. I begin to feel as though I should like to go home.

November 2

I received furlough for twenty days and start for home tomorrow.

November 8

I voted for Old Abe at the White Schoolhouse, Mason Township, Michigan.

1865

January 1

Welcome the new year, and may it be one of less bloodshed and strife but one of greater events, is, I hope, the prayer of every true American as well as my own. It is a pleasant day, but it is somewhat lonesome to me to be shut up in the smoky and muddy streets of Nashville. The ground is slightly covered with snow, but the ground is frozen beneath. The warm sun overhead has caused it to disappear, and in its stead we have mud. It is not much of a holiday here, and there seems to be but little doing in the narrow and crowded streets but the usual military and commercial business. For me, I have passed the time cleverly, but not pleasantly. I am feeling better tonight.

January 2

Another day of the new year has passed, and nothing

of interest save the usual transactions of business has graced the sunshine and mud of this city. I have tried to busy myself in various ways but have failed in all save that of writing. The time otherwise has been passed in idleness. Wes started for the regiment yesterday, and I wanted to go out but could not. I feel lonesome without his company, and indeed I am alone among strangers. I would give a good deal to be able to join my command, but I must remain here for a time. John Miller came to see me yesterday, but I was disappointed in not receiving the package he had for me, it being stolen.

January 4

The day has been warm and pleasant but of very little interest. Yesterday we were obliged to elbow our way through the crowded streets and gaze continually on the immense trains of government wagons that continually block the streets. Today it is the same. The pavements are crowded with footmen and the streets with wagons and carriages. I cannot read, and I must content myself with hearing what I can, and it is but mighty little. The Doctor made an application of nitrate of silver to my eyes this morning, and I have been mad at myself for allowing it to be done. I have sworn by all that is great and good that such treatment shall not be repeated.

January 8

This morning I mopped and made preparation for inspection. That over, B. More and I strolled about town.

We saw nothing inviting nor interesting save the funeral procession of a cavalry officer. That was the first time I had ever seen cavalry paying their last respects to a dead comrade. I met Colonel Shafer on the street but did not recognize him until he spoke to me. He was formerly of A Company of the 19th regiment Michigan but is now promoted to Colonel of the 28th Michigan. I had but little time to talk with him. His regiment (the 28th) was ordered to the Mississippi and was to start tomorrow morning. I wished him good luck, and we parted. The streets are crowded and muddy as usual, with rain falling almost constantly.

January 14

I had a rough night of it last night. I was attacked with pneumonia but have succeeded in breaking it up, and I feel much better today. I hope to feel better tomorrow.

January 23

This is pay day, and I have received $229.65. I also settled my clothing account to date of payment, December 31, 1864. Nothing further of interest has occured. The boys are spending their money freely, and their packets will be correspondingly lighter before many days. It snowed last night and has been a very disagreeable day so far. Tonight it is freezing and is by far the coldest night I have seen in Nashville. No time has been spared me today, and I am rather tired. I have been at the pay table all day and upon my feet, but I feel well and especially my eyes are doing well.

January 24

I have been relieved from duty today. I am therfore no longer a Bummer, but a patient, and what my destiny is God knows. One thing is certain—I am going to take things cool. I have busied myself today in sending home money and attending business of various kinds. Nothing worthy of note has transpired, save that the sun has shone all day, and the cold winter air has become more warm and pleasant.

January 28

Again today I have nothing of interest to note. I have received some mail today and have employed my time in reading and writing. For amusement, I went to the theatre in the evening, where was played "Dot, of The Cricket on the Hearth," with the farce of "The Fool of the Family." The former piece was very good, but the latter was a nuisance. I passed the evening pleasantly, because it was a deviation from the routine of hospital life.

February 2

The weather has changed again today, and it is now raining very hard. I have passed the time as usual, and nothing of interest has been noted save the arrival of the

4th Army Corps. Various rumors are afloat as to their objects, but none have any foundation to base their speculations upon. I had intended to go to the Orphans' Fair again tonight, but the sudden change of atmosphere has made my eyes worse, and I dare not venture out so far from the ward.

February 9

The day is characteristic of yesterday. I have passed the time as usual until evening, when I went to the theatre and listened to a play entitled "Putnam," or "The Iron Son of '76" and was very well entertained.

February 10

I again sought the theatre to listen to a play entitled "Eagle Eye" or "The Last of the Mohawks." There I found Captain M. B. Tice, who was once a Private of old Company E, 19th Michigan. I had a good time with him, and the visit paid quite as well as the theatre. The last time I saw him was at Camp Chase, Ohio, and last June I recorded his discharge in the company books, so I was surprised to find him at the theatre with a pumpkin vine on his shoulder.

February 20

The weather has been very pleasant for the last week, so much so that it has seemed like spring. I have done nothing today except nurse my teeth. I have had four

Downtown Nashville viewed from the Capitol

extracted, and, if they do not feel better tomorrow, I'll have them all extracted.

February 21

My teeth do not ache today, but my face is mighty sore. I have been out to Fort Negly and adjacent defenses and had a big tramp. I was in search of one D. Shoemaker, government employee, formerly an old friend, but did not succeed in finding him.

February 22

Nothing of importance has occurred here today, though it is the birthday of Washington. However, it has been a day of great rejoicing among the soldiers here. The receipt of news of the fall of Charleston caused great merriment, and one hundred guns were fired in honor of our forefather. Thus, it has been one continuous roar of artillery this afternoon. It has rained all day, so the citizens have had a very tedious day for the election to amend their state constitution.

March 4

The rain has subsided, but the river has overflown its banks, and the lower portion of the city is submerged. The boats land in the streets and deliver their cargo to the warehouse windows. The river is nearly two miles wide now, at least so the boys tell me. I know there is water as far as I can see. There is nothing else of interest. Aside from my ramble upon the river bank, I have passed the time as usual. This day Old Abe is again proclaimed president, but it is hardly thought of here. Also, Tennessee elects her governor and the free state tickets, but all is more quiet than a township election in Michigan. A national salute is being fired tonight in honor of the inaugural of Old Abe.

March 9

It is raining yet, and the flood has nearly reached the height it did in '47. In short, Nashville is now an island in the channel of the river. New troops are coming in as fast as ever, and the city is swarming with them.

March 13

The monotony was changed today by an examination by the Medical Board, but I am no wiser than before they made the examination. I suspect, however, that I was condemned and in due course of time will be turned over to the V.R.C. correl to wear a blue jacket. I do not fancy the idea, but it is only five months that I will have to serve, so I am not caring so much. I can't run away as I did at Camp Chase, for my regiment is too far off, so I have made up my mind to make the best of the next five months and do the duty that is set off to me.

March 14

The examination yesterday furnishes us a subject for amusement, and many a slur is thrown at one another about our dysentery blue, etc. I find there are about eight in the ward that were transferred, and the majority of them are expecting to go north. I am praying that their anticipation may be realized, but it is a good thing for me to speculate upon. The day is bright and warm, but the wind is blowing a perfect gale. There is no news from any quarter.

March 17

This is another beautiful day, but nothing unusual has occurred, save the promenade of the Order of Fenian Brotherhood. They have celebrated the day in great style and with success. The order was presented two beautiful flags (one of the U.S. colors, the other the flag of Ireland) by the Irish ladies of Nashville. Upon the whole, it was a fine affair. I have spent the time in rambling through different parts of the city, but have seen nothing new to note.

March 20

This day has been celebrated by the negroes of the city. A large number paraded the streets with music, badges and banners. On the latter were several mottoes. Among them were, "We Ask Not for Social but for Political Equality," "We Can Forget and Forgive the Past," etc. The crowd went to a grove in the suburbs to have their dinner and speaking, and the morning papers speak very highly of the affair. I only saw the procession pass through the street, and, to give my opinion, the nigger is getting mighty saucy, but I give them credit for good organization and order. I have spent the day about as usual for me. To relieve the monotony, I have received and perused one letter. There is no news.

March 23

Today I received two months' pay from Major Knapp and have had a little excitement with which to pass the day. As usual, there are some drunk ones after being paid.

March 24

I procured a pass today and have been promenading

all over the city. I purchased a pair of boots and returned to my quarters. I saw nothing new in my rambles, but on my return to the ward I think I have not seen as drunken a set of men in some time. Money is plentiful, and all kinds of Yankee notions can be seen in the ward. My observation is that many a dollar of the soldiers' money is spent foolishly here that is needed by their families at home.

March 26

I have sat about the ward all day and written one letter. My eyes are a good deal better today than they have been for the past week, and I am feeling quite proud over this fact. I shall expect every day of this week to hear from the examination I had two weeks ago, and possibly get started off for some northern point. It is warm and pleasant.

April 3

The Freeman's Legislature of Tennessee met at the state house early this morning and were drawing great crowds of people. When the glorious news of the fall of Richmond and Petersburg came, the state house was almost instantly deserted, and the people gathered in squads upon the streets to read the extras. Thousands of flags were flung to the breeze, a salute of artillery and musketry was fired, and the people were intoxicated with the good news.

April 5

The morning dawned bright and fresh. I saw Governor Brownlow inaugurated at the statehouse and listened to his address. Among the noted men present were Major Generals Thomas, Rousseau, and Milroy and a host of Brigadiers. There was the greatest enthusiasm. Still further out to the contraband camp, I found B. Shoemaker at work on the barracks. I had not seen him for about six years.

April 11

It continues raining. The telegraph bore to us the glorious news of the surrender of Lee's Army, and there is great rejoicing among the citizens. The soldiers make but a few demonstrations of their joy, though it is intense.

April 13

The day is bright and lovely again. At noon a salute was fired on the arrival of General Thomas from the front. There is no news save a few particulars from Richmond. I received a letter from the regiment.

April 14

It has the appearance of rain again today, but it is cool and pleasant. At noon a salute of heavy guns from

Lee's surrender to Grant

President Lincoln in Richmond the day after its fall, and eleven days before his own assassination

all the forts and musketry was fired in honor of the raising of the old flag over Fort Sumter by General Anderson. There was nothing else of interest. I am feeling much better. In fact, I am well, and I owe it to my own treatment. Preparations are being made for a great jubilee tomorrow over our recent victories, etc.

April 15

At early dawn troops began to move in different directions, and citizens began to assemble upon the sidewalks to celebrate the day. All was going off lively, and anticipations were running high for a grand time, when, with the speed of lightning, the news of the assassination of the President and the Secretary of State came upon us. The report was not credited at first, and all went forward gaily, but dispatch after dispatch finally forced it upon the minds of the people, and for a short time everything seemed to be spellbound. Not a word was spoken, not a command was given, not a person moved. At last the spell was broken. Flags were lowered to half-mast. The column of troops moved off with reversed arms and drooping march to the time of the dead march or funeral music. From this moment every countenance wore a look of sorrow. Even the merry youth of eight or nine summers wore a sad and mournful countenance as he carried his little draped flag in his hand. Flags were furled and draped in mourning, and many a building that was being prepared for illumination was draped and suddenly turned into a house of mourning. The procession dispersed, and citizens returned to their homes. At noon the streets were almost deserted, and every door was draped in mourning. The streets were again thronged at a late hour to hear and read the extras that had been published, and here again a new scene occurred. Every soldier's heart was fired with indignation, and the citizen partook of the spirit. Every man that rejoiced over the news was doomed to death on the spot. Some were shot, others bayonetted, others mauled to death. At this writing I learn of six or seven that have thus met their doom. Minute guns have been firing since noon, bells have been tolling, etc. For my part I have been silent and kept my temper, though it has been a hard blow, and it has been hard work to restrain my feelings. My friend D. Shoemaker paid me a visit this afternoon, but I was too sorrowful to enjoy it. I received several letters, too, but they too had lost in a measure their meaning and influence, so I will seek my virtuous couch to forget my sorrow in sleep.

April 16

It is unusually quiet today. Every one seems to be downhearted. Every one is mourning. The streets are deserted by everyone save the church going people and the patrol. No government wagons are to be seen upon the streets, that never before have failed to crowd the streets on the Sabbath. All departments of business are closed, and it seems like a Sunday at home and by far the gloomiest and most lonesome one to me that I have seen in the service. I have fought the dreaded battle on Sundays and witnessed my comrades fall all around me, but it has not made me feel half so badly as I do today.

The day is pleasant and inviting, but the national gloom destroys all its comforts. I have passed my time within the ward.

April 19

At nine o'clock the funeral procession began to form. First were the troops at the Post, next came the hearse, the convalescent and invalid soldiers, then the State Department, then the citizens in their different orders. Next came the negroes. The procession was very long, numbering about eight thousand, besides thousands of ladies upon the sidewalks. The line of march was through the principal streets to the suburbs south of the depot, where the troops formed in hollow square, with the hearse, Fire Department and Citizens within the square. There the funeral ceremonies were performed by Governor Brownlow and General Rousseau. Owing to the great number present, it was impossible to hear what was said. I returned to the ward about four o'clock the tiredest I have been since last summer's campaign, but well satisfied with the proceedings. It was the most solemn occasion I ever saw. I had the honor of Lieutenant commanding Company.

April 20

Hospital No. 8 is to be broken up today, and all morning I have been very busy in transferring the patients to different hospitals in the city. At noon I took leave of the hospital and soon found myself safely within the walls of the Cumberland Hospital, where I have good quarters in Ward 10. It is rather a nice place, and I am well pleased with my position, but have had no time to prospect and note the merits or demerits of the hospital. The day closed with a cool April shower.

April 22

Today I have passed my time in the yard, shoveling dirt, laying sod, etc. I am a little tired, but I feel the better for exercise. Too, I have read some and written a few letters. There is no news save the rumor of the surrender of Johnston to General Sherman. The day has been bright and lovely, though it was cool in the morning.

April 29

I am feeling pretty well again today, but I feel the effects of my cold yet. We have the official news today of General Johnston's surrender to General Sherman on the same terms granted Lee on the 23rd instant. The day has been cloudy but pleasant, and our hearts are filled with joy, which has been the substitute for sunshine.

April 30

There is an order from the War Department this morning directing that all convalescents in hospital be discharged, and it is upon every tongue that we will soon be going home. I can't see it yet but pray it may be so. Time only will tell how much of the order will be executed. I am all right today. I have been writing and receiving letters most of the time. The day has been cloudy but pleasant.

May 3

Today we were ordered to report to headquarters and hoped that it was for transfer north. All men that were examined by the same board were called for and transferred, but Sergeant Humphrey of the 125th Illinois and I were sent back to the ward to await further orders. I was disappointed, for I was somewhat anxious to get away from this place, but now I begin to think my fate is sealed, viz: That I shall remain here this summer. Sergeant Humphrey and I have sworn to make the best of the place together.

May 5

This is the twenty-fifth anniversary of my birthday, and, had it not been for my books and a letter, it would have been a very dull day. Though it has been very warm, it has been very pleasant. Stripped to the shirt and barefooted, I have been able to keep cool and enjoy my reading and writing.

May 7

Today has been one of more interest than common with me. The dedication of the Moorhead Chapel of the Cumberland Hospital was the program. The discourse was a good one and appropriate, but, as is always the case, the Christian Commission took too much credit upon themselves. The circumstances are as follows: Mrs. Moorhead, through the Christian Commission, donated $1,600 for building a chapel in this hospital. The government gave about $1,600 more to the enterprise, and the result is that they have a building worth, in ordinary times, not to exceed $300. It is nothing but a shell and not worth as much money as an ordinary 30x40 barn. The plea was that the Christian Commission had erected a place of worship worth $3,200, and the soldier ought to be thankful for it. I couldn't see it.

May 9

General Thomas reviewed the 4th Army Corps today almost within sight of the hospital, but we were not allowed the privilege of going to see the review. We could

hear them cheer as they passed. It is thus I feel the
tyranny exercised over me while in hospital. In short,
they would shave our heads, and I don't know but what
they would put striped clothes upon us, if they dared to.
I spent the day in reading, or, at least, a part of the
time. The rest of the time I listened to the music and
cheers of the army and longed for an hour of freedom
to go and see them.

May 11

Today commenced the discharging of patients under
the late orders from the War Department. I have been
put on duty at headquarters for that purpose. I have
discharged about thirty and feel somewhat tired, but it
has been a cool day to write.

May 12

I have been very busy indeed. I have written fifty
men's discharges and have had some rare sport. It seems
like old times to get on duty with my pen once more. I
have had no time to note anything outside of the office.

May 13

We have been very busy again today and discharged
some fifty men. I notice that each one's heart lightens
upon receiving his papers, and their countenances
brighten at the prospect of soon seeing home and
friends. It does me good to see them get their papers
and start for home.

May 16

This has been another busy day. I have made out another fifty discharges, but still the number of applicants does not decrease any. A nice little affair came off in the hospital at night. First was a volunteer concert, then refreshments by the Christian and Sanitary Commission, followed by a general jubilee. The former was very good and did great credit to the choir, the second was bountiful and was well conducted by the ladies of the Commission. The latter was for the most part a promiscuous affair. Several little spicy speeches were made by the Surgeon in Charge and others. The 15th U.S.A. Band gave some very good music. Although the boys enjoyed themselves, I must say that it seemed to me to be a kind of mockery. It is late, and I must retire.

May 17

Again today I have been writing and have been very busy, but as a reward I got my own discharge under way, and, if no misfortune happens to it, I will soon be a free man again. We have had some nice April showers today, and the air is cool and refreshing. In short, it has been a great day for business, and I can say that I have improved it.

May 18

It has been another cool and pleasant day, and business has progressed finely. We have finished discharging in the hospital. There are a good many left about the

To all whom it may Concern.

Know ye, That _Hamlin A. Coe_ a _Sergt_ of ~~Captain~~ Lieut _J M Alexander_ Company, (E,) 19 Regiment of _Michigan Infantry_ VOLUNTEERS who was enrolled on the _Sixth_ day of _August_ one thousand eight hundred and _sixty two_ to serve _Three_ years or during the war, is hereby **Discharged** from the service of the United States, this _Seventeenth_ day of _May_, 186_5_, at _Nashville Tenn_ by reason of _in accordance with instructions in telegram from War Dept — dated May 3 1865_ (No objection to his being re-enlisted is known to exist.)

Said _Hamlin A Coe_ was born in _Sandusky Co_ in the State of _Ohio_, is _Twenty one_ years of age, _Five_ feet _Seven½_ inches high. _Dark_ complexion, _Dark_ eyes. _Dark_ hair, and by occupation, when enrolled, a _Wagon Maker_

Given at _Nashville Tenn_ this _Seventeenth_ day of _May_ 1865.

J. W. Chickering
Capt 88 Ills S. V. & A. A. G. M.
~~Commanding the Dep't~~
2 Div 4 AC

* This sentence will be erased should there be anything in the conduct or physical condition of the soldier rendering him unfit for the Army.

H. S. O No 99.

Adam
_Co._

"As a reward, I got my own discharge under way."

hospital yet who will be discharged as soon as their descriptive lists arrive, and above all, I have received my discharge. I can hardly realize that I have so suddenly been transferred to a citizen, and I am afraid I shall get sick of my bargain before I get through with it. However, I shall try to get into God's country before I get disheartened. I left my papers at the Pay Department this afternoon and will get my pay on them tomorrow.

May 19

I settled with the U.S. in full, receiving $195.70 as my due at the Pay Department in the City of Nashville, but as there is a slight imperfection in my discharge, I shall have to remain here another day and possibly longer; but I have the advantage of them by settlement, and whether the papers are righted or not, this child is bound for home. I can hardly realize that I am a citizen, but, nevertheless, I am and must assume the position of one. It will not be until I can reach home in safety that I can realize the fact, where I hope my friends will help me to reclaim my position in society and throw off the habits of a soldier. It has been a cool, rainy day.

May 20

Early this morning I went to Captain Hough's office and had my discharge examined, but was obliged to leave it for Captain Chickering to correct when he came back from Chattanooga, but the polite Captain of the 19th U.S. gave me a certificate of discharge, so that I can go home and have my papers sent to me. Still another obstacle came up tonight that will keep me here some time. The late rains have washed away some of the bridges, so there are no trains running. I shall remain at the Cumberland Hospital tonight, and tomorrow, I hope, will see me on my way home.

May 21

Early this morning I started for the depot to take passage home but found the trains were not running, so I retraced my steps to Hospital No. 14 and spent the day. The trains will not run before Thursday next, so I have concluded to take river passage.

May 22

This morning I took passage upon the Marmora for Louisville, and at three o'clock was under way, but the boat is now moored at Clarksville for the night.

May 23

This morning I awoke to find the boat still moored at Clarksville, but by sunrise we were under way and going at a rapid speed down the current. Nine A.M. found us moored along the wild banks of the Cumberland taking on wood. At ten A.M. we were again moored at a little town by the name of Linton. One o'clock P.M. again found us moored and loading tobacco. At sundown we were under way again, but soon coming to another little town we moored to the landing. The trip thus far has been slow and tedious, too much so to be enjoyed. I should have noted that early this morning we passed the memorable Fort Donaldson. There is a new fort a little above the old one. Otherwise the scenery is the same. It is sixty miles to the Ohio.

May 24

At twelve o'clock midnight we were moored at the mouth of the Cumberland, and on waking this morning I found myself thirty miles up the Ohio. At nine o'clock we were at Caven Rock, Illinois. At three P.M. we were at Shawneetown, Illinois. Progress is rather slow. At five o'clock P.M. we passed the Wabash, and at sundown we touched at Uniontown, Kentucky, but only for a moment. Night closes around us, and we are plowing the muddy and swollen Ohio. It is very dark, and the boat is running very slowly. The ride begins to be somewhat tedious as well as monotonous.

May 25

It has rained all day. At four o'clock A.M. I awoke to find the boat moored at Evansville, Indiana, where they were discharging a cargo of tobacco. I went ashore and took some notes about the town. It is a very pretty place, and it seemed good to set foot on free soil once more a citizen, but we were off early for Louisville, Kentucky, distant two hundred miles. At two o'clock P.M. we moored to the Indiana shore and coaled. The steamer Huntsville came up and coaled at the same time but was off before us. At four o'clock P.M. we had overtaken the

Huntsville, and the two boats were on a race. The Marmora was on fire for a few moments but soon was all right and flying like the wind. At dark we came off winner of the race by two points on the bow.

May 26

I slept but little last night. It is cold and stormy. Four o'clock A.M. found us at Brandonsville, Kentucky, forty miles from Louisville. At ten thirty o'clock A.M. we were moored at the mouth of Salt River, Kentucky, to discharge a lot of Johnny passengers. The wind blew us hard ashore, and it was with some difficulty we got off. At two o'clock P.M. we were moored at the rapids two and one half miles below the city of Louisville. The boys were so tired of the boat that they left the boat and took the street car at Portland for Louisville. I put up at the National Hotel, ate supper and took passage upon a transfer for Jeffersonville. At ten o'clock P.M. I took passage upon the platform of a car for Indianapolis. It is quite cool, and there is a prospect of a hard night, but the train is crowded, and I was obliged to do the best I could.

EDITOR'S NOTE: *On this day Confederate General Kirby-Smith surrendered his army to the Union in Mississippi. The war was over.*

May 27

At five o'clock A.M. I arrived at Indianapolis and went

to the Hotel Golden Gate where I awaited breakfast. After breakfast I passed the time in prospecting and purchasing some clothes. At twelve thirty P.M. I was again on my way home via Lafayette and Salem Crossing, at which place I arrived at seven thirty P.M. At eight thirty P.M. I took passage upon a freight train for Elkhart.

May 28

I arrived at Elkhart at one thirty o'clock this morning and found the town deserted, or, rather, the good people had retired long before this late hour, and the quiet around me told me they were asleep. Passing along the street, I entered Faber's saloon (the only open door I could see in town) and there left my knapsack. I immediately set out for home on foot, where I arrived at daylight and had the pleasure of waking up the folks. I am so tired from the effects of my journey that I can hardly navigate today, but I am happy when I know that I am once more in God's country and a free man. I am feeling rather poorly, but with a little care I shall soon feel like a new man again.

Note: Whoever should read my diaries for the years of '62, '63, '64, and '65 will not criticize them, I hope, for they have invariably been written in a great hurry and often at great disadvantages, and, though brief and unmeaning to some who may read them, they contain a correct statement of my observations and actions while a soldier in the U.S. Army. Though I have omitted thousands of little incidents that have occurred during this time, they are as fresh in my mind as though the scenes were transacted but yesterday, and I hope I may

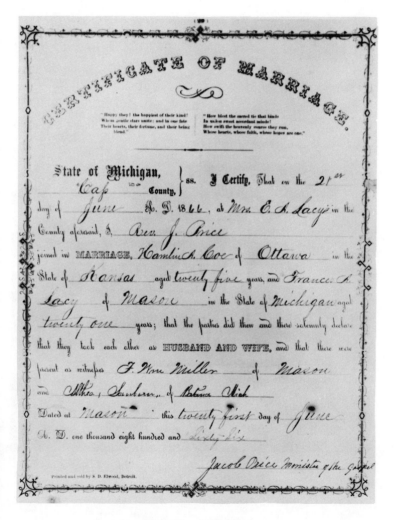

The Marriage Certificate

Frances Ann, just before her marriage to Ham Coe

find time to write them. My wish is now being gratified: that is, that I could fight the battles of my country and return to my home to write the closing remarks of my

soldier diary. And now I lay it aside for future reference, to enjoy the happy moments with friends and resume my place in society.

Ham Coe and family sixteen years after the war